The Unrealizable

THE ITALIAN LIST

GIORGIO AGAMBEN
The Unrealizable
Towards a Politics of Ontology

TRANSLATED BY
ALBERTO TOSCANO

LONDON NEW YORK CALCUTTA

THE ITALIAN LIST
Series Editor: Alberto Toscano

This book has been translated thanks to a translation grant awarded by the
Italian Ministry of Foreign Affairs and International Cooperation.

Questo libro è stato tradotto grazie a un contributo alla traduzione assegnato
dal Ministero degli Affari Esteri e della Cooperazione Internazionale italiano.

Seagull Books, 2025

First published in Italian as *L'irrealizzabile: Per una politica dell'ontologia*
© Giulio Einaudi editore s.p.a., Torino, 2022

First published in English translation by Seagull Books, 2025
English translation © Alberto Toscano, 2025

ISBN 978 1 80309 467 0

British Library Cataloguing-in-Publication Data
A catalogue record for this book is available from the British Library

Typeset by Seagull Books, Calcutta, India
Printed and bound in the USA by Integrated Books International

CONTENTS

The two texts that make up this book are autonomous, but the second—as has repeatedly happened to the author—originated, more or less consciously, with the aim of deepening and developing the theme on which the first text ended. The doctrine that reared its head there—on possibility as the cognition of a knowability and not of an object—corresponds, in the second essay, to the reading of the Platonic *chora*, of space-matter as the experience of a pure receptivity without object. These texts can thus be read in their continuity, as two attempts to restore thinking to its 'thing'. Philosophy is neither a science nor a theory calling for its realization, but a possibility that is already perfectly real, and, as such, unrealizable. The politics that abides by this possibility is the only true politics.

The Unrealizable

Threshold

1. The verb 'to realize' [*realizzare*] appears late in Romance languages—in Italian not before the eighteenth century, as the translation of the French *réaliser*. From then on, however, it has become increasingly more frequent, not only in the vocabulary of economics and politics, but also— especially in its reflexive voice—in that of personal experience. Giacomo Leopardi, though he often warns against the abuse of Gallicisms in Italian, employs the term and its derivative forms repeatedly, namely, regarding the recurrent theme of illusions (as he writes in the *Zibaldone*: 'Society in fact lacks the resources to realize illusions, insofar as they are realizable').[1] And if, in modernity, politics and art define the sphere in which illusions act with the greatest force, it is no surprise that it is in these domains that the lexicon of realization finds its greatest deployment.

---

1 Giacomo Leopardi, *Pensieri di varia filosofia e di bella letteratura* (*Zibaldone di pensieri*), VOL. 2 (Florence: Successori Le Monnier, 1898), p. 128 (§680). Unless otherwise specified, all translations from non-English sources are the translator's own.

2. It is common to ascribe to Marx the idea of a realization of philosophy in politics. In truth, the interpretation of the passages from the introduction to the *Critique of Hegel's Philosophy of Right* where he seems to advance this thesis is anything but obvious. He first formulates it as an objection to an unspecified '*practical* political party' that advocated the negation of philosophy. As Marx writes: 'You cannot abolish [*aufheben*] philosophy without realizing [*verwirklichen*] it.' Shortly after, against the representatives of the opposite party, he adds that they believed they 'could realize philosophy without abolishing it'.[2] And, after defining the proletariat as the dissolution of all ranks, the introduction concludes with the imperative affirmation that binds the realization of philosophy and the abolition of the proletariat into a circle: 'Philosophy cannot realize itself without the abolition of the proletariat and the proletariat cannot abolish itself without the realization of philosophy.'[3]

Earlier still, in the notes to the dissertation on the *Difference between the Democritean and Epicurean Philosophy of Nature*, which he defended at Jena in 1841, Marx had written that when philosophy tries to realize itself in the world, 'the becoming philosophical of the world is

---

2 Karl Marx, *Early Writings* (Rodney Livingstone and Gregor Benton trans.) (London: Penguin, 1992), pp. 249–50. [Translation modified: Livingstone and Benton here render *aufheben* as 'transcend'. All quotations in the present volume have been reproduced in British spelling for consistency.]

3 Marx, *Early Writings*, p. 257 [translation modified].

also the becoming worldly of philosophy, while its realization is also its loss [*ihre Verwirklichung zugleich ihr Verlust*].'[4] Since Marx did not intend here simply to reprise the Hegelian dialectic unchanged, it is not at all obvious what he might have meant by a revolution that would have verified the two symmetrical theses 'abolish and realize philosophy' and 'abolish and realize the proletariat'. It was by playing on this lack of clarity that Adorno could open his *Negative Dialectics* with the assertion that 'Philosophy, which once seemed obsolete, lives on because the moment to realize it was missed.'[5] Almost as if, if it hadn't missed that moment, it would no longer exist; as if, by realizing itself, it would have abolished itself. But what does 'realizing' oneself mean? And what would it mean to 'miss one's own realization'? We use these terms as though their meaning were self-evident—but as soon as we try to define realization, it escapes us, revealing itself as opaque and contradictory.

3. In the *Phenomenology of Spirit*, the two German terms for realization, *Verwirklichung* and *Realisierung*, appear respectively 49 and 19 times, while there are about 20 instances of the verb *realisieren*. Even more frequent are

---

4 Karl Marx and Frederick Engels, *Collected Works, Volume 1: Marx, 1835–1843* (London: Lawrence and Wishart, 1975), p. 85 [translation modified].

5 Theodor W. Adorno, *Negative Dialectics* (E. B. Ashton trans.) (London: Routledge, 1973), p. 3.

the two words for 'reality': 68 cases of *Wirklichkeit* and 110 of *Realität*. As has been noted, this frequency is not accidental; we are dealing with terms that fully belong to Hegel's technical vocabulary.[6]

The experience of consciousness that is at stake in the *Phenomenology* implies a continuous process of realization, which is nevertheless invariably defective or unattained each and every time. Whether we are dealing with sense-certainty (in which the reality it believes it's affirming 'abolishes its truth,' such that it 'is saying the opposite of what it wants to say'),[7] with the 'dialectic of force' ('[t]he realization of force is also at the same time the loss of reality'),[8] with 'natural consciousness' (for which 'the realization of the concept will count instead, to it, as the loss of itself'),[9] with culture (in which '[t]o itself, the self is only actual as *abolished*'),[10] with the beautiful soul (whose realization 'vanishes like a shapeless vapor'),[11] or with the unhappy

6 Joseph Gauvin, 'Les dérivés de "Res" dans la *Phénomenologie de l'esprit*' in Marta Fattori and Massimo Luigi Bianchi (eds), *Res: III Colloquio Internazionale del Lessico Intellettuale Europeo (Roma, 7–9 gennaio 1980)* (Rome: Edizioni dell'Ateneo, 1982).

7 G. W. F. Hegel, *The Phenomenology of Spirit* (Terry Pinkard trans. and ed.) (Cambridge: Cambridge University Press, 2018), p. 66.

8 Hegel, *Phenomenology of Spirit*, p. 85.

9 Hegel, *Phenomenology of Spirit*, p. 52.

10 Hegel, *Phenomenology of Spirit*, p. 286 [translation modified: where Agamben opts for 'abolished' (*abolito*), Pinkard gives 'sublated'].

11 Hegel, *Phenomenology of Spirit*, p. 381.

consciousness ('its *reality* is, to itself, immediately a *nullity*'),[12] realization is always also the loss and abolition of self. Each of the figures in which spirit realizes itself in its movement abolishes itself to make room for another figure, which in turn suppresses itself into another until we reach the final figure: 'absolute knowledge' (*das Absolute Wissen*). But insofar as spirit is nothing but this movement of unceasing self-realization, its 'last figure' (*letzte Gestalt*) cannot but take the form of a remembrance 'in which spirit forsakes its existence and gives its shape over to recollection', something like 'a gallery of pictures, of which each [is] endowed with the entire wealth of spirit.' In recollection, spirit 'has to begin all over again without prejudice in its immediacy, and, from its immediacy, to rear itself again to maturity, as if all that had preceded it were lost to it.'[13] Absolute knowledge (that is, 'spirit that knows itself as spirit')[14] is not a 'reality' but the contemplation of an unceasing 'realization', whose reality must therefore be denied each and every time and appear in recollection only as the 'foam of its infinity'.[15] Realization is the most radical negation of reality, because if everything is realization, then reality is something insufficient, something that must be ceaselessly abolished and overcome, and the final

12 Hegel, *Phenomenology of Spirit*, p. 131.

13 Hegel, *Phenomenology of Spirit*, p. 466.

14 Hegel, *Phenomenology of Spirit*, p. 395.

15 Hegel, *Phenomenology of Spirit*, p. 467 [translation modified].

figure of consciousness cannot but take the form of a realization of realization (this is absolute knowledge). Against this conception, we must recall that reality is not the effect of a realization but an inseparable attribute of being. The real, as such, is by definition unrealizable.

4. It is remarkable that almost a century later, Guy Debord will reprise Marx's formula but with reference to art, not philosophy. Debord chides the Dadaists for having wanted to abolish art without realizing it and the surrealists for having wanted to realize art without abolishing it. As for the situationists, they intend instead to realize art and, at the same time, abolish it.

The verb, which in Marx's text we have translated as 'abolish'—*aufheben*—is the same which, with its double meaning, plays a crucial function in Hegel's dialectic: to abolish is to make something cease (*aufhören lassen*) and to conserve it (*aufbewahren*). Art can be realized in politics only if it somehow abolishes and conserves itself within it. As Robert Klein observed in an essay from 1967, tellingly entitled 'The Eclipse of the Work of Art',[16] the abolition that the avant-gardes envisaged was not directed so much

---

16 Robert Klein, 'The Eclipse of the Work of Art' in *Form and Meaning: Writings on the Renaissance and Modern Art* (Madeline Jay and Leon Wieseltier trans) (Princeton, NJ: Princeton University Press, 1981), pp. 176–83.

against art as against the work, which art then claimed to outlive. This remainder of wandering arthood is seized upon by contemporary art, which relinquishes the reality of the work in the name of the realization of art within life.

The verb *aufheben*, to which Hegel entrusts this dialectical arcanum, acquired its twofold meaning through Martin Luther's translation of the New Testament. Faced with the passage from the Letter to the Romans (3:31) which had always confounded interpreters—because Paul seems to affirm both the abolition of the law and its confirmation ('Do we then abolish [*katargoumen*] the law through faith? God forbid: yea, we establish [*histanomen*] the law')— Luther decides to translate the antinomic gesture of Pauline *katargesis* with *aufheben* (*heben wir das Gesetz auf*).

But the apostle's intent was perforce more complex. In the messianic perspective in which he placed himself, the advent of the Messiah meant the end of law (*telos tou nomou*; Romans 10:4), in the twofold sense that the term *telos* carries in Greek: end as well as achievement, fullness. Paul's critique was not aimed in fact at the *Torah* itself, but at the law in its normative aspect, which he unequivocally defines as *nomos ton entolon* (law of commands; Ephesians 2:15) or *nomos ton ergon* (law of works; Romans 3:27). In other words, he is calling into question the rabbinical principle according to which justice is only obtained by carrying out the works that law prescribes ('For we maintain that a person is justified by faith apart from the works of the law'; Romans 3:28).

This is why, every time he needs to express the relationship between the Messiah and the law, Paul employs the verb *katargeo*, which does not mean 'destroy'—as the Vulgate sometimes translates—but 'I render inoperative, I take out of the *ergon* and *energeia*' (in this sense, *katargeo* is the opposite of *energeo*, which means 'I put into operation, I enact'). Paul is perfectly aware of the opposition—so familiar to Greek thought after Aristotle—between power (*dynamis*) and act (*energeia*), and he refers to it repeatedly (Ephesians 3:7, 'through the working [*energeia*] of his power [*dynamis*]'; Galatians 3:5, the spirit 'puts into operation [*energon*] in you the powers [*dynameis*]'). Regarding law, however, the messianic event operates an inversion of the normal relationship between the two terms, which privileges the act; the fulfilment of the law that takes place here instead deactivates *energeia* and makes its commandments inoperative. Law ceases to be something that must be realized in facts and works and the *katargesis* of its normative aspect reveals to the believer the real possibility of faith, as fullness and achievement of the *Torah*, which now presents itself as 'law of faith' (*nomos pisteos*; Romans 3:27). In this way, law is restored to its power—a power which, according to the limpid terms of 2 Corinthians 12:9, 'is made perfect in weakness' (*dynamis en astheneia teleitai*). We cannot properly speak here either of abolition or realization: faith is not something that can be realized because it is the only reality and the only truth of law.

5. An insufficiently attentive reading of his *Seventh Letter* would suggest that, in his three Sicilian voyages to the court of Dionysus, Plato was seeking to realize philosophy in politics. In effect, Plato justifies his sojourn with the tyrant with the fear of appearing in his own eyes as a man 'of mere words reluctant to embark upon any action', and avows that he succumbed to the entreaties of his friends, who reminded him that 'if ever an attempt was to be made to put into practice [*apotelein*] my convictions about law and government, now was the time.'[17] What he meant by these words can only really be grasped by comparing them with what he writes a little earlier about the correct relation between philosophy and politics: 'the evils that afflict human generations will never cease until either true and genuine philosophers attain political power or the rulers of states by some divine dispensation genuinely do philosophy [*philosophesei*].'[18] This lapidary thesis reprises the theory of the philosopher-king that Plato expounds in almost identical terms in a famous passage from the *Republic*:

17 Plato, *Letter VII* in *Phaedrus and Letters VII and VIII* (Walter Hamilton trans.) (London: Penguin, 1973), p. 118 (328c).

18 Plato, *Phaedrus and Letters VII and VIII*, p. 116 (326b) [translation modified].

Until philosophers rule as kings or those who are now called kings and leading men genuinely and adequately philosophize [*philosophesosi gnesios te kai ikanos*], that is, until political power and philosophy entirely coincide [*eis tauton sympesei*—the expression is significant: *sympegnymi* also means 'to coagulate'—G. A.] [...] cities will have no rest from evils [...] nor, I think, will the human race. And, until this happens, the politics we've been describing in theory will never be born [*physei*] to the fullest extent possible or see the light of the sun.[19]

The leading interpretation of this Platonic thesis is that the philosophers must govern the city because only philosophical rationality can suggest the correct measures that must be taken by those governing. In other words, Plato would be affirming that good government is that which realizes and puts into practice the ideas of philosophers. A variant of this interpretation is already present in the passage from Hegel's *Lessons in the History of Philosophy* in which he reads the philosopher-king of the *Republic* in the following terms:

---

19 Plato, *Republic* (G. M. A. Grube and C. D. C. Reeve trans) in *Complete Works* (John M. Cooper and D. S. Hutchinson eds) (Indianapolis, IN, and Cambridge: Hackett, 1997), p. 1100 (473d).

Plato here plainly asserts the necessity for thus uniting philosophy with political power. As to this demand, it may seem a piece of great presumption to say that philosophers should have the government of states accorded to them, for the territory or ground of history is different from that of philosophy. In history, the Idea, as the absolute power, has certainly to realize itself; in other words, God rules in the world. But history is the Idea working itself out in a natural way, and not with the consciousness of the Idea. The action is certainly in accordance with universal reflections on right, conformity with custom, and subordination to divine will; but we must recognize that action represents at the same time the endeavours of the subject as such for particular ends.[20]

The philosopher-king is that sovereign who borrows from philosophy the universal principles of rationality and lets them prevail over any particular end: 'when Plato says that philosophers should rule, he signifies that the whole life of the state must be regulated according to universal principles.'[21]

---

20 G. W. F. Hegel, *Lectures on the History of Philosophy, Volume 2: Plato and the Platonists* (E. S. Haldane and Frances H. Simson trans) (Lincoln, NE, and London: University of Nebraska Press, 1995), p. 24 [translation modified].

21 Hegel, *Lectures on the History of Philosophy*, VOL. 2, p. 26 [translation modified].

We are indebted to Michel Foucault for having shown the inadequacy of these interpretations of Plato's theorem, which unjustifiably equate it with the Aristotelian thesis of the philosopher as advisor to the sovereign. What is decisive here is only the coincidence of philosophy and politics in a single subject. As Foucault observes:

> What is important [. . .] is the fact that someone who practices philosophy is also someone who exercises power. However, from the fact that the person who practices philosophy also exercises power, and the person who exercises power is also someone who practices philosophy, we cannot at all infer that his knowledge of philosophy will be the law of his action and political decisions. What matters, what is required, is that the subject of political power also be the subject of a philosophical activity.[22]

It is not simply a matter of making a philosophical knowledge coincide with a political rationality; what is in question is rather a mode of being or, more precisely, for the individual who does philosophy, 'a way for the individual to constitute himself as a subject on a certain mode of being.'[23] In other words, what is at stake is the

---

22 Michel Foucault, *The Government of Self and Others: Lectures at the Collège de France, 1982–1983* (Graham Burchell trans., Frédéric Gros ed.) (Basingstoke: Palgrave Macmillan, 2010), p. 294.

23 Foucault, *Government of Self and Others*, p. 294.

identity between the mode of being of the philos-
ophizing subject and the mode of being of the subject practicing politics. If kings must be philosophers it is not so they will be able to ask their
philosophical knowledge what they should do in
a given set of circumstances [. . .] there is no
coincidence of content, no isomorphism of ration-
alities, no identity of philosophical and political
discourse, but rather an identity of the philos-
ophizing subject with the governing subject.[24]

If we try to develop Foucault's reflections in the direction
that interests us here, we must begin by asking ourselves
what it means, in Plato's words, for the *dynamis politiké*,
political power, to coincide with philosophy, and vice versa.
As Foucault has shown, we are certainly not dealing with
the realization of the one in the other, but with their coincidence in the one and the same subject. At the beginning of
the *Seventh Letter*, Plato recounts how he had decided to
devote himself to philosophy after recognizing that any
political activity in his city had become impossible—that,
in other words, the possibility of philosophy coincided with
the impossibility of politics. In the philosopher-king, the
possibility of philosophy and that of politics coincide, 'by
some divine dispensation', in a single subject. The philosopher does not thereby stop being a philosopher, he does
not abolish himself by realizing himself in philosophy, but

---

24 Foucault, *Government of Self and Others*, pp. 294–95.

his power comes to be identified with that of the sovereign. The coinciding of these two powers is the reality and truth of both. Insofar as they are real, they do not need realization; on the contrary, they are, properly speaking, unrealizable.

This is why, as Pierre Hadot has observed, while Aristotle's school shaped one for the philosophical life— for the way of life of the theorist as distinct from that of the sovereign, whom the philosopher could advise, if needs be—Plato's Academy had an essentially political end, but only to the extent that it aimed to make the philosopher's mode of being coincide with that of the king. In the *Seventh Letter*, Plato explicitly warns against the idea that the philosopher can turn into the king's advisor without the latter changing his mode of being:

> When a man is sick and following a course injurious to his health, surely the first task of anyone whom he consults must be to change his way of life [*metaballein ton bion*]? [. . .] But if those who consult him have completely abandoned the true principles of government and firmly refuse to return to the right track, and tell their adviser to let politics alone on pain of death and to confine himself to advising on the quickest and easiest way for them to obtain the permanent satisfaction of their wishes and desires, I should call the person who gave advice on these terms a coward.[25]

25 Plato, *Letter VII*, pp. 121–22 (330d–331a) [translation modified].

Philosophy must not try to realize itself in politics: if it wants the two powers to coincide and the king to become a philosopher, it must instead always turn into the guardian of its own unrealizability.

Giorgio Pasquali concludes his extremely insightful reading of the *Seventh Letter* with a long excursus on *tyche*, which repeatedly appears in Plato's reflections as an irrational, hostile and maleficent power, but at times also as a 'divine' and 'beneficent' power, as the *theia moira* (divine dispensation), which in the above-cited passage (326b) makes it so that philosophers attain power in the city. From the start, recalling the trial against Socrates, he writes that it took place *kata tina tyche*, by some chance (325b5), just as, shortly after, the collapse of the hopes pinned on Dion happens by dint of a 'demon or something maleficent [*tis daimon e tis alitherios*]'.[26] Pasquali shows how the problem of *tyche* is also central in the oldest dialogues and especially in the *Laws*. If, in the *Republic*, the reasonable man does not agree to involve himself in the politics of his city 'unless some divine good luck chances to be his [*theia . . . tyche*]',[27] in the *Laws*, the Athenian guest, before expounding his own ideas about legislation, utters the melancholic theorem according to which 'no mortal ever passes any law at all, and [. . .] human affairs are almost entirely matters of chance [*tychas*]'.[28] Pasquali speaks, in this regard, of a 'demonological dualism' in Plato's thought, according to which

---

26 Plato, *Letter VII*, p. 128 (336b) [translation modified].

27 Plato, *Republic*, p. 1199 (592a).

28 Plato, *Laws* (Trevor J. Saunders trans.) in *Complete Works*, p. 1396 (708e) [translation modified].

human vicissitudes appear as a battle in which man is aided or thwarted by supernatural entities.[29]

As so often in Plato, what we are dealing with is really a myth, which in this instance is the site of a confrontation with a particularly thorny problem for an ancient mind: the problem of contingency. The series of events which happen to human beings is not a necessary course that can be accounted for through causal explanations that refer back to the infinite nor, as in Hegel, by a process in which spirit realizes itself in each and every case. The ultimate meaning of events escapes us and *tyche*—which means 'event'—is the name of contingency, of the pure and, in the final analysis, inexplicable coming to presence of something—*contingit*, that is to say, 'happens'. Historical events depend, in the final analysis, on *tyche*, and that is also why the philosopher-king cannot claim to realize philosophy in his actions. Plato is, in this regard, closer than Hegel to the results of the science of our own time, which leaves ample room for chance and contingency.

6. A critique of the concept of realization in the sphere of politics is contained in Walter Benjamin's 'Theological-Political Fragment', which editors date to the early 1920s but which its author considered so important as to convey it to Adorno in their final meeting in Sanremo at the beginning of 1938 as 'absolutely new'.

---

29 Giorgio Pasquali, *Le lettere di Platone* (Florence: Le Monnier, 1938; 2nd EDN: Florence: Sansoni, 1967).

The theoretical problem of the fragment is that of the relationship between the profane order and the Kingdom, between history and the messianic, which Benjamin defines without reservations as 'one of the essential teachings of the philosophy of history'.[30] This relationship is even more problematic inasmuch as the fragment begins by unreservedly asserting the radical heterogeneity of the two elements. Since only the Messiah completes (*vollendet*, 'brings to its end') historical happening, and both redeems and produces the relationship between historical happening and the messianic,

> nothing that is historical can relate itself, from its own ground, to anything messianic. Therefore, the Kingdom of God is not the telos of the historical dynamic; it cannot be established as a goal. From the standpoint of history, it is not the goal [*Ziel*] but the terminus [*Ende*]. Therefore, the secular order cannot be built on the idea of the Divine Kingdom, and theocracy has no political but only a religious meaning.[31]

The kingdom—and the Marxian concept of a classless society which, as we read in Benjamin's eighteenth thesis

---

30 Walter Benjamin, 'Theological-Political Fragment' in *Selected Writings: Volume 3, 1935–1938* (Howard Eiland and Michael W. Jennings eds, Edmund Jephcott, Howard Eiland et al. trans) (Cambridge, MA: Harvard University Press, 2002), p. 305.

31 Benjamin, 'Theological-Political Fragment', p. 305.

on the philosophy of history, is its secularization—is not something that can ever be posited as the goal of a political action and be 'realized' through a revolution or a historical transformation. In the perspective of the 'Fragment', one may then say that the error of modern ideologies has consisted in flattening the messianic order onto the historical order, forgetting that the Kingdom, to maintain its proper efficacy, can never be posited as a goal to be realized, but only as a terminus (*Ende*). If it is posited as something that must be realized within the profane historical order, it will end up fatally reproducing the existing order in new forms. Classless society, revolution and anarchy are, in this sense, like the Kingdom, messianic concepts which cannot become goals without losing their proper force and nature.

This does not mean that they are ineffective or devoid of meaning on the historical level. Between them and the profane sphere there is indeed a relation, but paradoxically it only results from the obstinate perseverance of each of the two orders in the direction that defines them. Thus, while the order of the profane 'should be erected on the idea of happiness', 'the immediate messianic intensity of the heart, of the inner man in isolation, passes through misfortune, as suffering.'[32] According to the exemplification suggested by Benjamin, their divergence is a genuine opposition and yet this opposition produces something like a relation:

---

32 Benjamin, 'Theological-Political Fragment', p. 305.

If one arrow points to the goal towards which operates the Dynamis of the profane acts, and another marks the direction of messianic intensity, then certainly the quest of free humanity for happiness diverges from the messianic direction. But just as a force, by virtue of the path it is moving along, can augment another force on the opposite path, so the profane order of the Profane promotes the coming of the Messianic Kingdom.[33]

Though it is in no way 'a category of [the] Kingdom', the Profane acts as a principle that facilitates 'its most unobtrusive approach'.[34]

Just as philosophy neither can nor should realize itself in politics but is already fully real, and just as, according to Paul, the obligation to realize the law through works does not produce justice, so in the 'Fragment' the messianic acts within historical happening only by remaining unrealizable within it. Only in this way does it shelter possibility, its most precious gift, without which no space could be opened for gesture and the event. We must stop thinking of the possible and the real as two functionally connected parts of a system that we can call the ontological-political machine of the West. Possibility is not something that must, by passing to the act, realize itself; on the contrary,

---

33 Benjamin, 'Theological-Political Fragment', p. 305 [translation modified: the English translation has 'secular' where Agamben opts for 'profane'].

34 Benjamin, 'Theological-Political Fragment', p. 305.

it is the absolutely unrealizable, whose reality, complete in itself, acts like a terminus (*Ende*) upon the historical happening that has petrified itself into facts, namely, by breaking and annihilating it. This is why Benjamin can write that the method of world politics 'must be called nihilism'.[35] The radical heterogeneity of the messianic does not allow for plans or calculations aimed at its fulfilment [*inveramento*] in a new historical order, but can appear in the latter only as an absolutely destituent real instance. And we define as destituent a power [*potenza*] that never lets itself be realized in a constituted power [*potere*].

---

35 Benjamin, 'Theological-Political Fragment', p. 306.

CHAPTER ONE

Res

1. According to lexicographers, the Latin word *res*, from which our terms reality and realization derive, is the most frequent term in the Latin literature that has come down to us. However, it is uniquely isolated in the classical Latin lexicon because the adjective *realis* and the adverb *realiter*, which derive from it, only appear from the fourth and fifth centuries of our era, while the noun *realitas* and the rare verb *realitare* (or *realitificare*) never feature before the late Middle Ages. Even more remarkable is the fact that this term, so frequent in Latin, is not conserved as such in modern languages, except for in French in the form *rien*, meaning 'nothing'. In its place, Romance languages employ a term derived from *causa*: *cosa* (thing), *chose*, *coisa*. The reason for this replacement of one term with another is genuinely semantic. In effect, even before signifying an object or a possessed good, *res* is the affair of human beings,

that which concerns them or is at stake for them and between them and which is thus almost synonymous with *lis* in the juridical sense, namely, what is at stake in a trial (Varro: 'therefore men between whom a matter was in dispute, called this a "suit" [*quibus res erat in controversia, ea vocabatur lis*]').[1] This is why from *res* the ancients derived *reus*, 'the one whose affairs are the object of a trial'; for the same reason, the word is often used adverbially in a causal sense: *quare*, *quam ob rem* (because of that thing, by cause of) and tends customarily to settle into a syntagmatic union with adjectives, to the point of almost disappearing into them: *res publica*, *res divina*, *res familiaris*, *res militaris*, *res adversae* or *secundae*. The original meaning of 'what concerns me, what is in the sphere of my interest' is evident in the expressions, already common in Plautus, *rem gerere*, *rem agere* (dealing with a matter), *rem narrare* (exposing a question).

The meaning of 'good, possessed thing', which the lexicons register as ancient next to that of 'affair', is actually derived from the latter. If in Plautus we thus encounter *res* as synonym of *pecunia*, this is because money is plausibly the paragon of 'what interests me'. Again, in Plautus, in euphemistic expressions like *mala res*, 'the ugly thing', to designate the whip with which the slave will be thrashed, the objectual meaning is secondary with respect to the

---

1 Varro, *On the Latin Language* (Roland G. Kent trans.) (London: William Heinemann Ltd, 1938), p. 347 (7.93).

'ugly business' that awaits him, just as the *res venerea* is not a thing but the complicated matter of love and sex.

It is noteworthy that philosophical reflection influenced the progressive decline of the 'affair of men' in the objective sense. In Lucretius, already in the title *De rerum natura*—absent from the manuscripts but present as a syntagm in the text and corresponding to the *peri physeos* of the Greek philosophers—*res* takes on the philosophical meaning of 'entity', which it will retain throughout the Latin world. The way in which the meanings of the term are tightly entangled in a semantic constellation where 'entity', 'thing' [*cosa*], 'cause' [*causa*] become indistinguishable is testified by a passage from the Lucretian poem on which it is worth reflecting:

> Thus too, if all things are create of four [*quattuor*
>   *ex rebus si cuncta creantur*]
> And all again [*res omnia*] dissolved into the four,
> How can the four be called the primal germs
> Of things [*rerum primordia*], more than all things
>   themselves be thought,
> By retroversion, primal germs of them?[2]

---

2 Lucretius, *Of the Nature of Things: A Metrical Translation* (William Ellery Leonard trans.) (London, Paris and Toronto: J. M. Dent & Sons Ltd, 1916), p. 29.

It is possible that among the factors that facilitated the semantic drift of the term in the direction of *ens* was the ever more frequent use of *res* in the negative expression *nulla res* as synonym of *nihil* (for instance, in Lucretius 1.150: *nullam rem e nihilo gigni divinitus umquam* [nothing is ever created by divine power out of nothing]): *res*, as entity, is the opposite of nothingness (whence the use of *nullius rei* as genitive of *nihil*). A passage from Cicero's *Topica* informs us about a first scission of *res* that anticipates the medieval one between *res extra animam* and *res in intellectu*, depending on whether the term is used for things that exist (*earum rerum qui sunt*) or for intelligible ones that are devoid of corporeal substance (like *usucapio, tutela, agnatio*).[3]

It is not by chance that Cicero's examples are drawn from the sphere of law. The philosophical meaning continues to be shadowed by the juridical meaning (in which

---

3 'Of definitions there are two prime classes, one defining things that exist [*earum rerum quae sunt*], and the other, things which are apprehended only by the mind [*earum quae intelleguntur*]. By things that exist I mean such as can be seen and touched: for example, farm, house, wall, rainwater, slave, animal, furniture, food, etc.; [. . .] On the other hand, by things which do not exist I mean those which cannot be touched or pointed out, but can, for all that, be perceived by the mind and comprehended; for example, you might define acquisition by long possession [*usus capionem*], guardianship [*tutelam*], *gens*, agnation; of these things there is no body, but a clear pattern and understanding impressed on the mind, and this I call a notion.' Cicero, Topics in *On Invention. The Best Kind of Orator. Topics* (H. M. Hubbell trans.) (Cambridge, MA: Harvard University Press, 1949), pp. 398–401 (5.27). [Trans.]

res, as evinced by the *Corpus iuris civilis*, is what enters in some way into the domain of law, whether it be a legal case, a possessed or alienated good—*res data*, *res adquisita*—or one bequeathed by inheritance—*res hereditaria*) and the political one, in which (as in the opening words of the work in which Augustus recounts his deeds) the *Res gestae* designate the actions carried out by the *imperator* in the exercise of his functions.

Res, like being, is the thing of human beings, the 'thing' of their thought and language, what provokes and concerns them in every way. The etymology—familiar to the ancients, uncertain for the moderns—from *reor* ('I think, count, judge'), seems to confirm this. But precisely insofar as it coincides with the entire sphere of human thought and action, the 'thing' will in each case have to divide and articulate itself in keeping with a variety of meanings and strategies, among which the mind risks getting lost.

In his lecture on 'The Thing', held at the Bavarian Academy of the Fine Arts in 1950, Heidegger outlines a brief genealogy of the German word *Ding* and its Latin equivalent *res*. Both originally mean, as we have already recalled, 'that which concerns human beings, an affair [*Angelegenheit*], a contested matter [*Streitfall*], a case at law [*Fall*]'.[4] This original meaning is supplemented in Latin

---

4 Martin Heidegger, 'The Thing' in *Poetry, Language, Thought* (Albert Hofstadter trans.) (New York: Harper & Row, 1971), p. 173 [translation modified].

by another, utterly different one, which replaces the first to the point of completely occluding it:

> The Latin word *res* denotes what pertains to man, concerns him and his interests in any way or manner. That which concerns man [*das Angehende*] is what is real in *res*. The Roman experience of the *realitas*[5] of *res* is that of a bearing-upon, a concern [*der Angang*]. But the Romans never properly thought through the essence of what they thus experienced. Rather, the Roman *realitas* of *res* is conceived in terms of the meaning of *on* which they took over from the Greek philosophy; *on*, Latin *ens*, means that which is present in the sense of standing forth here [*Herstand*]. *Res* becomes *ens*, that which is present in the sense of what is produced and represented. The authentic *realitas* of *res*—originally experienced by the Romans as a bearing-upon or concern—remains, as essence of the present thing, buried. Conversely, in later times, especially in the Middle Ages, the term *res* serves to designate every *ens* qua *ens*, that is, everything present in any way whatever, even if it stands forth and presences only in mental representation as an *ens rationis*. The same happens with the corresponding German term *dinc*; it denotes anything whatever that is in any way.[6]

At this point, Heidegger abandons the genealogy he had briefly sketched out to return to the example of the 'thing' with which

---

5 Heidegger here anachronistically anticipates the use of the term *realitas* which the Romans, as we've seen, did not know.

6 Heidegger, 'The Thing', pp. 173–74 [translation modified].

he'd opened his lecture: a jug. Definitively turning his back on the 'thing' of the ontological tradition, notwithstanding his familiarity with it, he opts for a regime of thinking which he himself—in the 'Letter to a Young Student' appended to the essay—regards as tainted by 'lawless caprice'.[7] The jug from which I drink to slake my thirst is not a thing in the sense of the Roman *res*, nor in that of the *ens*, conceived after the medieval fashion; now it is inserted in the 'fourfold' of earth and sky, divinities and mortals, the relation of which constitutes its essence. Our aim here is to take up this abruptly interrupted philosophical genealogy of the thing.

2. It is in medieval philosophy that the semantic evolution of *res* towards the ontological meaning of *ens* attains its utmost development. At the end of the ancient world, in Augustine, the domain of *res* is already defined in its full amplitude by opposition with that of language and signs:

> All instruction is either about things or about signs; but things are learnt by means of signs. I now use the word 'thing' in a strict sense, to signify that which is never employed as a sign of anything else: for example, wood, stone, cattle, and other things of that kind.[8]

---

7 Heidegger, 'The Thing', p. 184.

8 Augustine of Hippo, *On Christian Doctrine* (J. F. Shaw trans.) (Mineola, NY: Dover, 2009), pp. 2–3 (1.2.2).

While it is important to note that—in keeping with a semantic drift that will always remain present even if rarely thematized—'thing' is here everything that is signified by language, the term's inherent ambiguity persists, for things too can be used as signs, like 'the wood which we read Moses cast into the bitter waters to make them sweet.'[9] Inversely, signs themselves, as far as their sensible aspect is concerned, are things, otherwise they could not exist (*quod enim nulla res est, omnino nihil est* [every sign is also a thing; for what is not a thing is nothing at all]).[10] The fact that the semantic sphere of the term is already so vast as to be identified with being is shown by how Augustine, conceding that 'it is not easy to find a name that will suitably express so great excellence', calls the Trinity itself 'thing':

> The true objects of enjoyment [*res ergo, quibus fruendum est*], then, are the Father and the Son and the Holy Spirit, who are at the same time the Trinity, one Being, supreme above all, and common to all who enjoy Him, if He is a thing, and not rather the cause of all things, or indeed even if He is the cause of all.[11]

---

9 Augustine, *On Christian Doctrine*, p. 3 (1.2.2).

10 Augustine, *On Christian Doctrine*, p. 3 (1.2.2).

11 Augustine, *On Christian Doctrine*, p. 4 (1.5.5) [translation modified].

From this moment onwards—also with respect to this problematic passage in Augustine—the dogged efforts of the theologians focus on defining the meaning of *res* with respect to the vocabulary of ontology. In the dislocation of *res* towards the dimension of being, the original meaning of 'what is at stake for someone' will be fractured by the scissions that govern Western ontology: being and entity, essence (*quidditas*) and existence, power and act, possibility and reality, *ens in intellectu* and *ens extra animam*, and the most common term—the thing, the 'affair' of speaking humans—will be marked by the same ambiguity that defines the use of the term 'being': both what is most abstract and the most immediate and tangible reality; what is simply possible in the minds of men and what exists in fact (*realiter*).

The prevailing tendency will be that of reserving for *res* the meaning of essence and power. As the Lateran Council of 1215 decreed: *illa res videlicet substantia, essentia sive natura divina* ('each of the three persons is that entity, namely, substance, essence or divine nature'; Canon 2). Or, as we read in a definition by Siger of Brabant (*Metaphysica*, IV): 'thing and entity [*res et ens*] signify the same essence but are not synonymous terms [. . .] entity signifies in the mode of the act [*per modum actus*], thing in the mode of habit [*per modum habitus*]';[12] habit is the

---

12 Siger of Brabant, *Quaestiones in Metaphysicam* (Armand Maurer ed.) (Louvain-la-Neuve: Institut supérieur de philosophie, 1983), p. 398; quoted

mode in which power or possibility habitually exists in a subject. Likewise, Thomas Aquinas, quoting Avicenna, affirms that *res* and *ens* are distinguished by whether we consider the essence of a thing or its existence.[13] It is even more remarkable that the adjective *realis* and the adverb *realiter* tend instead to take on the meaning—which they will retain in post-medieval and modern usage—of 'objectively existent' (Aquinas can thus define creatures as 'real expressions' [*realis quaedam expressio*] of what is conceived in the divine Word).[14]

Yet the other meanings of the term *res* do not disappear. A philosophical lexicon from the fourteenth century, which reprises the formulae used by Bonaventure in his *Commentary on the Sentences*, inventories the semantic sphere of the term as follows: '*res* is said in three ways'—in the first sense, the common (*communiter*) one, which is made to derive from *reor*, it signifies 'everything that falls under knowledge' (*omne illud quod cadit in cognitione*); in

---

in Jacqueline Hamesse, 'Res chez les auteurs philosophiques des XII et XIII siècles ou le passage de la neutralité à la specificité' in Fattori and Bianchi (eds), *Res*, p. 99.

13 See Thomas Aquinas, *Commentary on the Sentences*, BOOK 1, DIST. 25, QUES. 1, ART. 4. ['Therefore for the same reason the three persons should not be called 'three beings' or 'three things' since the term 'being' (*ens*) is drawn from existence (*esse*), and the term 'thing' (*res*) from whatness/essence (*quidditas*), as Avicenna [*Metaphysics* 4.5] says. (*Ergo eadem ratione non debent tres personae dici tres entes vel tres res; cum nomen entis imponatur ab esse, et nomen rei a quidditate, ut dicit Avicenna.*)']

14 See Thomas Aquinas, *Summa contra Gentiles*, BOOK 4, CHAP. 42.

the second, which is the 'proper' (*proprie*) one, it is identified with the entity outside the soul (*convertitur cum ente
extra animam*); in the third and 'most proper' (*magis proprie*), it is said 'only of the entity as such, namely, substance'
(*de ente per se, quod est substantia*).[15]

Because it names the 'thing' of thought and knowledge
insofar as it is traversed by a series of splits and articula-
tions, the term *res* will never lose its ambiguity and will
thereby condition the vocabulary of ontology and the 'reality' of being that is at stake within it. In the dual etymology
that Aquinas suggests for *res*, the splitting between an existence outside the soul and a solely mental reality is plainly
attested: 'the name of the thing has a twofold origin: both
from what is in the soul—and in this sense *res* derives
from *reor, reris* [thinking, reckoning]—and from what is
outside the soul, and in this sense it signifies something
fixed [*ratum*] and stable in nature.'[16]

3. A significant moment in the term's history is the inclu-
sion of *res* among the concepts that medieval logic defines
as transcendent or transcendental, namely, *ens, unum,
verum, bonum, perfectum*, namely, extremely general concepts that transcend the categories and can be predicated
of any of them. The origins of the problematization of these

15 Quoted in Hamesse, '*Res* chez les auteurs philosophiques', p. 93.

16 Aquinas, *Commentary on the Sentences*, BOOK 1, DIST. 25, QUES. 1, ART. 4.

concepts are to be sought in the theological discussions of the twelfth century on the *quaestio* of whether general terms like *ens*, *res*, *aliquid* can apply equally to God and creatures.[17] The decisive influence of the introduction of *res* among the transcendentals—and into the medieval ontological vocabulary more generally—is owed, however, to Avicenna [Ibn Sina] (or, more precisely, to the translation of Avicenna into Latin, which spread throughout Europe in the final decades of the twelfth century). In a passage from the *Liber de philosophia prima* constantly cited by those who identify with both the ancients and the moderns,[18] Avicenna had affirmed the primacy of the notions of 'thing' (*res*; Arabic: *shay*) and 'existent' (*ens*; Arabic: *mawgud*), insofar as they are originary and immediately knowable (*statim imprimuntur in anima prima impressione*), not derivable from others (*quae non acquiritur ex aliis notionibus*), and not definable save in a circular manner (*nullo modo potest manifestari aliquid horum probatione quae non sit circularis*).

17 Luisa Valente, '*Ens, unum, bonum*: Elementi per una storia dei trascendentali in Boezio e nella tradizione boeziana del sec. XII' in Stefano Caroti, Ruedi Imbach, Zénon Kaluza, Loris Sturlese and Giorgio Stabile (eds), '*Ad ingenii acuitionem*': *Studies in Honour of Alfonso Maierù* (Louvain-la-Neuve: Brepols, 2006).

18 Avicenna, *Liber de philosophia prima* (S. Van Riet ed.) (Leiden: Brill, 1977), pp. 31–32 (1.5).

If, as has been noted,[19] the two concepts are extensionally identical, they are nevertheless intentionally distinct, namely, according to their way of signifying: *res* refers to essence or quiddity, while *ens* instead concerns things considered as existent. Each thing, Avicenna writes, has a *certitudo* (Arabic: *haqiqa*, 'reality or truth') through which it is what it is: 'just as a triangle has a *certitudo* that defines it as a triangle and whiteness has a *certitudo* that constitutes it as whiteness.'[20] He thus fashions from *shay* the term *shay'iyya*, literally 'thingness' (or 'thinghood'), which curiously Latin translators do not render as *realitas*, as we may have expected, but as *causalitas*. We owe to Marie-Thérèse d'Alverny an incisive hypothesis.[21] Translations from Arabic to Latin were two-handed, in this case by a Sephardic Jewish scholar, Avendauth [Abraham ibn Daud]—who knew Arabic and translated word by word into Spanish or Italian and who had likely rendered *shay'iyya* by *cosidad* or *cosalità*—and by Domingo Gundisalvi (Gundissalinus). The latter, transcribing into Latin, mistook *cosidad* or *cosalità* for *causalitas*. Because of this error of translation, the word for 'thingness', which had been invented in Arabic by

---

19 Robert Wisnovsky, 'Notes on Avicenna's Concept of Thingness (*šay'iyya*)', *Arabic Sciences and Philosophy* 10 (2000): 189–90.

20 Avicenna, *Liber de philosophia prima*, pp. 34–35 (1.5).

21 Marie-Thérèse d'Alverny, 'L'Introduction d'Avicenne en Occident', *La revue du Caire*, Millenaire d'Avicenna (special issue) (1951): 130–39. Reprinted in *Avicenne en Occident: Recueil d'articles de Marie-Thérèse d'Alverny réunis en hommage à l'auteur* (Paris: Vrin, 1993), pp. 12–16.

Avicenna, was not transmitted to Romance languages at the moment of the reception of his thought into Latin culture. Without this mistake, today we would say 'thingness' and not 'reality' and perhaps everything would be clearer.

If it is beyond doubt that, as Heidegger has reminded us, the philosophical vocabulary of the West was formed through a series of mistranslations, it is equally certain that in Avicenna 'thing' is constitutively an ambiguous concept. On the one hand, it designates the primordial experience from which all knowledge is born; on the other, it signifies essence or quiddity, as though the 'thing' preceded the distinction between essence and existence, while at the same time partaking of it. The most recent studies have in fact shown that both the primacy of essence over existence and the ontological status of the thing—two correlated doctrinal points that the hermeneutic tradition ascribes to Avicenna—are really in his thinking far more complex problems than an initial reading might suggest. Avicenna is aware that the 'thing', insofar as it names the primordial element at the basis of every true utterance (*res est id de quo potest aliquid vere enuntiari*) is presupposed by every utterance and is always already included in any definition that may be given of it.

> When you say that the thing is that of which something can be legitimately uttered, it is the same as if I said that the thing is the thing of which something can be legitimately uttered [*res est res de qua*

vere potest aliquid enuntiari], because 'this', 'that'
and 'thing' signify the same, and so in the definition of the thing you would have placed the thing
[*nam et id et illud et res eiusdem sensus sunt. Iam
igitur posuisti rem in definitione rei*].[22]

This is why Avicenna can affirm that the thing is not sep-
arable from existence, 'because the intellection of existence
constantly accompanies it [*quoniam intellectus de ente
semper comitabitur illam*]' and 'if it were not considered as
existent it would not be a thing [*si autem non esset ita,
tunc non esset res*]'.[23]

The hypothesis that we wish to advance is that *res*, 'the
thing', names—in a culture that cannot yet thematize language as such—the pure intentionality of language, namely,
the fact that every utterance refers to something. That is
why *res* is necessarily presupposed by every discourse—
and thus also by every statement about the thing. Consider
the passage we already quoted from the *Liber de prima
philosophia* in which Avicenna defines essence: 'each thing
has a *certitudo* through which it is what it is' (*unaquaeque
res habet certitudinem qua est id quod est*). If the thing is
here evidently presupposed by the essence that characterizes it, this is not because it designates (as will be the case
in Kant) the existent object of a perception, but because it
is the name of the intentional correlate of language, prior

---

22 Avicenna, *Liber de philosophia prima*, p. 34 (1.5).

23 Avicenna, *Liber de philosophia prima*, p. 36 (1.5).

to the distinction between essence and existence (in later Scholasticism, expressions such as *essentia rei* and even *existentia rei* will become common, without questions being raised about the ontological status of *res*, since both essence and existence, through which the thing is defined, refer to it). Examples could be easily multiplied, for instance, a few lines earlier, the passage in which Avicenna defines the thing as that which is most immediate and common ('What can most easily be imagined on its own [*Quae autem sunt promptiora ad imaginandum*] is what is common to all *things* [*quae communia sunt omnibus res*] such as the *thing*, the existent, the one and the like [*sicut res et ens et unum et cetera*]')[24] where the repetition 'thing/thing' betrays the breadth as well as the ambiguity of the term's meaning.

If we cannot speak of the 'thing' without repeating and presupposing the word 'thing,' it is because *res*, like other transcendental predicates, names the very intentionality of language: *res* is the thing of language, the 'real' correlate of every discourse and every intellection. This allowed later philosophers like Francis of Marchia and Henry of Ghent to draw from Avicenna the consequence that *ens*, as concomitant to the concept *res*, is posterior to it and cannot therefore be the first object of metaphysics (*ergo intentio entis, cum non sit prima intentio, non erit primum subiectum*

---

24 Avicenna, *Liber de philosophia prima*, p. 33 (1.5).

Metaphysicae).[25] And when Henry of Ghent, in order to define 'the thing or something' (*res sive aliquid*) as 'that which is most common to all', must oppose it to the 'pure nothing' (*purum nihil*)—because only the thing is by nature in relation with the intellect—what he is really defining is the very intentionality of language. Thought, like language, always implies the reference to a 'thing' and a thingness and never a 'nothing' (*nihil est natum movere intellectum nisi habens rationem alicuius realitatis* [nothing can move understanding unless it has a relation to some reality]).[26]

But it is equally true that the thing, as soon as it is named as such, immediately splits into 'what it is' (*quid est, essentia, quidditas*), on the one hand, and its simple existence (*quodditas* or *anitas*, the 'if it is'), on the other. This split of the thing is coextensive with Western ontology, in its triumphs as well as its aporias. Or rather, it constitutes the secret motor of what we could call the ontological machine of the West.

25 Francisci de Marchia (Francis of Marchia), '*Questiones in Metaphysicam, I, q. I*' in Albert Zimmerman (ed.), *Ontologie oder Metaphysik: Die Diskussion über den Gegenstand in Metaphysik im 13 und 14 Jahrhundert* (Leuven: Peeters, 1998), p. 66.

26 Henry of Ghent, *Quodlibet VII* (G. A. Wilson ed.), Opera Omnia, VOL. 11 (Leuven: Leuven University Press, 1991), 'QUAESTIONES 1 et 2', pp. 26–27.

It has been noted that in the passage from Henry of Ghent, *res* signifies everything that is not nothing and therefore implies a level of abstraction that verges on tautology.[27] In truth, what is at stake in Henry's definition of *res sive aliquid* is the fact that language (and thought, *intellectus*) always refers to something and never to nothing, namely, a kind of answer *avant la lettre* to Leibniz's question: 'why is there something rather than nothing?' There is something rather than nothing because thought can only correspond to something *habens rationem alicuius realitatis*, regardless of whether inside or outside the mind. If, as Jean-François Courtine has suggested, the term *res* designates here 'the content of any representation whatever, abstracting from its reality *extra intellectum*, but not from "reality" understood as the consistency proper to the *cogitabile* or to thought,'[28] what is here thought *a parte obiecti* is the very intentionality of thought and language, opposed to nothingness, to the *purum nihil*. As Suárez will elaborate: *Nihil dicimus, cui nulla respondet notio* [we do not say anything that does not correspond to an idea], while the something (*aliquid*) is *cui aliqua notio respondet*.[29] (Modern thought begins instead with Leonardo da Vinci's thesis according to which language always implies a reference to nothingness: 'What is called nothing is found only in time and words.')[30]

---

27 Olivier Boulnois, 'L'invention de la réalité', *Quaestio* 17 (2017): 145.

28 Jean-François Courtine, *Suarez et le système de la métaphysique* (Paris: Presses universitaires de France, 1990), p. 184.

29 Courtine, *Suarez*, p. 252.

30 Leonardo da Vinci, Codex Arundel (British Library Arundel MS 263), fol. 131*r*.

The classic precursor of the Arab-medieval concept of thing is likely the *ti*, the 'something' that the Stoics considered as the highest genus, more general than being. It is possible, as has been suggested, that Aristotle's late commentators, like Alexander of Aphrodisias and Simplicius, served as intermediaries between the Stoics and the Arabs. It is worth considering the critique levied at this notion by Alexander (who, like Plotinus, was a sworn adversary of the Stoa):

> Here we can demonstrate how much the Stoics err in arguing that the something [*ti*] is the genus under which the existent must be subsumed: if it is something, it will also be an existent; if it is an existent, then it will be definable as existent. They try to evade this dilemma by affirming that existent is said only of bodies and they argue that the something is a higher genus because it is predicated both of incorporeals and corporeals.[31]

In truth, by referring the *ti* also to incorporeals, which can be named and thought without existing as bodies in reality, the Stoics seem implicitly to consider *ti* as the correlate of thought and language—similar, in this sense, to the *cogitabile* as the super-transcendental of Scholasticism.

---

31 Alexander of Aphrodisias, *In Aristotelis Topicorum: Libros Octo Commentaria* (Max Wallies ed.), Commentaria in Aristotelem Graeca, VOL. 2, PART 2 (Hermann Alexander Diels series ed.) (Berlin: Reimer, 1891), 4.1–9.

4. In an important essay, Jean Jolivet has shown that the distinction between essence and existence in Avicenna does not stem solely from Aristotle's *Metaphysics* (which, according to legend, Avicenna read forty times), but is decisively influenced by the theological discussions of the *mutakallimum* on the relation between thing and existence in the Quran.[32] In the Quran, we can indeed read God addressing the thing, saying: 'be'. This, according to the commentators, seemed to imply the unacceptable consequence that *shay*, the thing, pre-existed God. Moreover, in the vocabulary of the Arab grammarians, the thing designated the subject of a predicate and, insofar as attributes are predicated of God, he (as had happened to Augustine, who had called the trinity 'thing') had to be considered as a 'thing'. Yet between the thing and the theological problem there was another, more decisive connection. Before Avicenna, al-Farabi, distinguishing between existence (*al-mawgud*) and the thing (*shay*), had already noted that the distinction cannot take place within God. In Avicenna, this theme returns forcefully, as it will do with equal vigour among Christian theologians: if the division between essence (thingness or reality) and existence, between possibility and actuality, dominates the knowledge of everything

---

32 Jean Jolivet, 'Aux origins de l'ontologie d'Ibn Sina' in *Philosophie médiévale arabe et latine* (Paris: Vrin, 1995), pp. 221–36; originally published in Jean Jolivet and Roshdi Rashed (eds), *Études sur Avicenne* (Paris: Les Belles Lettres, 1984), pp. 11–28). [The *mutakallimum*, the masters of *kalam* (word, discourse, speech), refers to medieval Muslim theologians. —Trans.]

that is not God, within the First Principle it must cease. The difference is really grounded in theology and only in a theological perspective does it take on its true meaning. These distinctions can obtain within creatures only because they coincide in God, and vice versa, they coincide in God so that they may be separated in creatures. In the *dispositif* of Western ontology, being is split into essence and existence, but this fracture finds in God both its presupposition and its composition. If the human mind can grasp and dominate reality only by sundering it into two distinct planes, their originary unity and possible rearticulation find in God their guarantee.

The distinction between essence and existence among Arabic philosophers is complicated by the fact that while in Greek the verb *einai* has both an existential [*esistentivo*] meaning ('God is') and the value of the grammatical copula ('God is good'), Arabic lacks the verb being in its copulative function ('Zaid is good' and 'Zaid is' imply the use of two different verbs); therefore, as has been noted, for Arabic philosophers, Aristotle sometimes speaks of existence and sometimes of essence, but never of being as such.[33]

---

33 A. C. Graham, 'Being in Linguistics and Philosophy: A Preliminary Inquiry', *Foundations of Language* 1 (1965): 223–31.

5. In Avicenna, the problem of modality is crucially important for a correct understanding of the relation between
essence and existence. In his thought, in keeping with a
process that will find its full expression in Scholasticism,
possibility tends to superimpose itself on essence, and the
act and necessity on existence. Olga Lizzini has shown that
if essence is in itself possible and the First Principle is what
gives it existence, 'then what Avicenna calls "thing"
becomes necessary by virtue of another thing.'[34] If creation
(the passage from essence to existence) is conceived as a
passage from potentiality [*potenza*] to the act, then possibility or potentiality becomes an obscure ontological presupposition prior to creation. Even if possibility (or essence)
were conceived as something existing in the divine intellect,
creation could not account for the origin of the possible
and it would no longer be a *creatio ex nihilo*, but a *creatio
ex possibili*.[35] If Avicenna at times seems to conceive creation according to the model of the artist, in which possibility precedes its realization in the mind, at other times
creation takes place outside of time, absolutely from
nothingness, without any transit from potential to actual.
In any case, when Scholasticism, following in Avicenna's
footsteps, will identify essence with possibility and existence
with the act, it will therewith necessarily inherit a series of

---

34 Olga Lizzini, 'Wuğūd-Mawğūd / Existence-Existent in Avicenna: A Key
Ontological Notion in Arabic Philosophy', *Quaestio* 3 (2003): 124.

35 Lizzini, 'Wuğūd-Mawğūd': p. 125.

aporias, which will reach critical mass in the ontological argument, that is, in the problem of the transit from essence to existence and from the power to the act of God.

6. The ambiguity of the word *res* is also borne by the term that derives from it, which, beginning in the twelfth century, will play an essential function in the philosophy of the West: *realitas*, reality (which to an ear accustomed to Latin would have sounded like 'thingness' to ours). Olivier Boulnois, who rightly defines it as a 'medieval invention',[36] recalls that a seventeenth-century lexicon (Étienne Chauvin's *Thesaurus philosophicus*)[37] already attributed its origin to Duns Scotus and his school, curiously adding that '*realitas* is a diminutive of *res*' and that the Scotists, who invented the word, distinguished it from *res*, considering it as 'something less than a thing' (*aliquid minus re*).[38]

Scotus in effect distinguishes the concept of reality (*realitas*) from that of *res*, but not as a simple diminutive or generic term; just as in whiteness (*albedo*) it is possible to make

---

36 Boulnois, 'L'invention de la réalité': 133.

37 Étienne Chauvin, *Thesaurus philosophicus* (Rotterdam: Pieter van der Slaart, 1692).

38 Boulnois, 'L'invention de la réalité': 134.

out different degrees of colour, so in a *res* one may distin-guish multiple *realitates* (in one thing multiple 'thinghoods' or modes of being a thing). *Realitas* expresses the degree of being of something (*gradus intrinsecus rei*—later Scotus will prefer to speak of *modus intrinsecus*, of *realitas formae* and *formalitas*). As we read, in agreement with Scotus, in Johannes Micraelius' *Lexicon philosophicum*, from which Chauvin's *Thesaurus* draws: 'reality is something in the thing [*realitas est aliquid in re*]. Therefore, in each thing we can find several realities and the realities must be dis-tinguished from the thing in which they are. So, in man we find rationality, animality and substantiality.'[39] These *realitates* are distinct—and here the terminological ambi-guity is particularly glaring—not *realiter* (that is, as things, *res*) but only *formaliter*.

Between real distinction, which takes place between one thing and another, and the distinction of reason, which is only in the mind, Scotus had in fact introduced formal distinction, which is something less than real distinction and more than a distinction of reason. It is thanks to this distinction that in one and the same thing there can be plural *realitates*, just as in one and the same man there is both genus and specific difference and in God both divinity and paternity.

---

39 Johannes Micraelius, *Lexicon philosophicum terminorum philosophis usitatorum*, 2nd EDN (Szczecin: Jeremiah Mamphras, 1661[1653]), col. 1203. Quoted in Boulnois, 'L'invention de la réalité': 134.

Formal distinction also makes it possible to understand how Scotus conceives of singular existence. In man, common nature and the difference that individualizes him are not two things, but two realities in the same thing (*realitates eiusdem rei*) that are only formally distinct (*formalitater distinctae*). Scotus can thus articulate in a new and ingenious way the difference between essence and existence: existence is not distinguished from essence like one thing from another (*res et res*), it is only the ultimate realization (*ultima realitas*, which Scotus sometimes calls haecceity, *haecceitas*) of common nature or essence. It 'is not assumed from an added form but from the ultimate reality of form [*numquam sumitur a forma addita, sed praecise ab ultima realitate formae*].'[40] Existence is not something that is added to essence but its ultimate reality, the last degree of form. In the words of Scotus, this ultimateness of form is its real perfection (*perfectio realis*), which as such is irreducibly simple (*simpliciter simplex*).[41]

Res and *realitas*, the 'thing' and its 'thinghood,' are tightly related and yet they do not coincide. Nothing is more real than *res* and yet *realitas* implies and perfects it. Whether—in keeping with the dominant tendency of medieval thought—essence prevails over existence and thingness over the thing, or whether one affirms the opposite, in every case the genealogy of our concept of reality leads us up to the threshold of a fundamental split.

---

40 Duns Scotus, *Ordinatio*, BOOK 2, DIST. 3, PART 1, QUES. 6, NOTE 180.

41 Scotus, *Ordinatio*, BOOK 1, DIST. 3, PART 1, QUES. 3, NOTE 159.

That Scotus' thought was decisively influenced by Avicenna is—
at least ever since Étienne Gilson's studies—indisputable.
Curiously, this is not the case for the concept of *realitas* which,
for the reasons adduced by d'Alverny, is rare in Latin translations
of Avicenna. However, it appears twice in the *Liber tertius natu-
ralium de generatione et corruptione*, not as a translation of
shay'iyya but of *al-wugud*, existence.

7. The most accurate translation of the term *realitas* in
Scotus is arguably not 'reality' but 'realization'. The *realitates*
that inhere in *res* express various degrees or levels of realization (*perfectio*) of essence. This realization should not
be conceived as the addition of a quidditatively distinct
form, like a thing is distinct from another (as form is added
to matter, for instance) but as the realization of a single *res*.
In whiteness, Scotus writes, there is no composition of one
thing and another; there are instead two different degrees
of reality (*duae realitates formales*) 'one of which is of the
genus realizable [*perfectibilis*] through the reality of difference.'[42] It is significant that Scotus compares ultimate reality
to a *quasi actus*, 'which determines the almost possible and
potential [*quasi possibilem et potentialem*] of the species.'[43]
Yet the passage of power into act is not undertaken here by
another form or essence, but from the realizing of form

---

42 Scotus, *Lectura*, BOOK 1, DIST. 8, PART 1, QUES. 3, NOTE 103.
43 Scotus, *Ordinatio*, BOOK 2, DIST. 3, PART 1, QUES. 6, NOTE 180.

itself, from an *ultima realitas formae* that brings about its *perfectio realis*. This is why Wolter was right to observe that the object of metaphysics for Duns Scotus was not simply the entity, but the 'existable', namely, a possibility that is always in the act of realizing itself in being.[44]

It is likely that the Scotist conceptualization was influenced by Avicennian emanationism, itself derived from the Neoplatonic *proodos* (procession). We have shown elsewhere,[45] in the footsteps of a study by Heinrich Dörrie, how the term *hypostasis*, which entered into the vocabulary of ontology with Neoplatonism, does not simply designate existence but existence as 'realization', and how its introduction profoundly alters the Aristotelian distinction between essence and existence. While in Aristotle essence was what resulted from a question aimed at grasping existence, existence as hypostasis is a performance and realization of essence. This is also the case for medieval thought, whose links with Neoplatonism are—also by way of Arabic mediation—as strong as those with Aristotelianism. One of the consequences of being's split into essence and existence, possibility and reality, is that existence now presents itself as the result of a process of realization variously conceived. Existence thus becomes a 'realization'—a hypostasis—of

44 Allan B. Wolter, *The Transcendentals and Their Function in the Metaphysics of Duns Scotus* (New York: St Bonaventure, 1946), p. 69.

45 Giorgio Agamben, *The Use of Bodies: Homo Sacer IV, 2* (Adam Kotsko trans.) (Stanford: Stanford University Press, 2016), p. 135.

essence. And when the term *hypostasis* enters the theological vocabulary to define the trinity (*mia ousia, treis hypostaseis*, which the Latins will translate by *una substantia, tres personae*), the meaning of the word, as Gregory of Nyssa details, is 'hypostatization according to essence' (*kat'ousian* [...] *hyphestosa dynamis*), namely, a realization of essence.

8. It is instructive to track the history of the term 'reality' among Scotus' disciples. In the *Tractatus de formalitatibus* attributed to Francis of Meyronnes, one of Scotus' most acute disciples, his teacher's concept of *realitas* is pushed in the direction of 'realization' to such an extent that Francis was compelled to coin the verb *realitare* (sometimes in the form *realizare* or *realificare*). This might be the first appearance of a term which, starting with Descartes, will have a rich future ahead of it in modern philosophy. 'Reality', we read in its commanding definition, 'is the intrinsic mode through which is realized everything that is in something [*realitas est modus intrinsecus mediante qui realitantur omnia quae sunt in aliquo*].' Francis coherently distinguishes three acceptations of the term 'thing': as substrate (*per modum substrati*), as predicate (*per modum praedicati*) and, lastly, the one according to which 'quiddity realizes itself through reality' (*quidditas realizatur per realitatem*).[46]

---

46 Francis of Meyronnes (Franciscus de Mayronis), *Tractatus formalitatum* in *In Libros Sententiarum, Quodlibeta, Tractatus formalitatum, De primo principio, Terminorum theologicalium declarationes, De univocatione*

He distinguishes in the same way the *substantia qualificata*, which is the substrate of the accidents, from what he calls *substantia realificata*, and further distinguishes within the latter between the essence contracted through haecceity (*quidditas contracta per hecceitatem*), existence itself, and the *realitas* through which existence has realized itself.

If it is true, as Boulnois suggests, that the birth of the concept of reality must be sought in the twelfth-century debate on the status of the formal distinction between essence and existence, it is equally important to recall that this is why the concept of reality is inseparable from a modal process of realization (from possible existence to necessary existence). We can therefore say that the first effect of the split in the thing of thought is that all of reality is transformed into a realization, and being itself is nothing but a process in which a possible is unceasingly realized.

A Franciscan theologian, Petrus Aureolus (Peter Auriol), professed against Scotus an original doctrine, which ended up denying the distinction between *realitas* and *res*, between essence and existence. It is significant that in order to negate the distinction he was obliged to bend the ontological terminology of his time, affirming, in something like a play on words, that *Nulla res*

(Mauritius de Hibernia ed.) (Venice, 1520), p. 264r; reprinted in Caroline Gaus, *Etiam realis Scientia: Petrus Aureolis konzeptualistische Transzendentalienlehre vor dem Hintergrund seiner Kritik am Formalitätenrealismus* (Leiden and Boston: Brill, 2008), p. 70.

differt realiter a realitate sua, 'no thing differs really [in a thingly way] from its reality [thinghood]. If it differs, it would be another reality, and therefore not its reality' (*Comm. Sent.,* dist. 3, par. 4, n. 31–32). Here too the meaning of the sentence is clarified if we translate *realitas* as realization: no thing differs from its realization in existence.

9. That at its birth the concept of 'reality' implies the modal meaning of realization and, at the same time, a constitutive connection with the divine creation of the world is evident from what is perhaps the first occurrence of the term, in Odo of Tournai's *Expositio in canonem missae* (eleventh century). Implicitly evoking the Prologue to the Gospel of John, Odo writes:

> It has been made from nothing and yet was in the word [*factum est de nihilo, erat tamen in verbo*]. It was made in a creaturely way [*crealiter*], and yet is eternally [*aeternaliter*]. It was in the supreme art [*in summa arte*], it was made in the thing [*in re*]; it lived in the reason of its maker formally [*formaliter*—or, following another possible version: *formabiliter*, in a formable or realizable manner—G. A.*]. It sprung from nothing [*de nihilo prodiit*] to be substantially what had been made. It lived in the word to be formally before it was substantially.[47]

47 Odo of Tournai, *Expositio in canonem missae,* DIST. 3 in *Patrologia Latina,* VOL. 160 (Jacques-Paul Migne ed.) (Paris: Garnier, 1880), col. 1060A.

Reprising the Augustinian paradigm of the *arca in arte* and the *arca in opera*,[48] Odo articulates the two moments of creation (in form and in substance, in the word and in the creature) as a process of realization that goes from possibility in the mind of the maker to substantial reality. If it is true that the centrality of the concept of creation defines the novelty of the Christian conception of the world, it is no less decisive for the history of the West that reality thereby becomes the fruit of a continuous process of realization. The word realizes itself in the world and the latter is consequently nothing but the ceaseless becoming real of the word. The fact that *creatio divina* is thereby thought by theologians as a *creatio continua*, without which creatures would be annihilated, confirms the inseparability between creative process and reality. The technological transformation of nature whose unlimited deployment we are witnessing today would be unthinkable if reality had not been conceived from the outset as a *realitas* and the latter as a creation and realization.

---

48 Augustine of Hippo, *In Johannis Evangelium Tractatus*, TRACT. 1, §17. 'A carpenter makes a chest. First he has the chest in his creative knowledge. For if he did not have the chest in his creative knowledge, from what source would he produce it in constructing it? [. . .] The chest in the product is not life; the chest in the creative knowledge is life. For the soul of the craftsman, in which exist all these things before they are produced, has life. [*Faber facit arcam. Primo in arte habet arcam. Si enim in arte arcam non haberet, non esset ut fabricando illam proferret . . . arca in opera non est vita, arca in vita est; quia vivit anima artificis, ubi sunt ista omnia antequam proferantur*]' *Tractates on the Gospel of John 1–10* (John W. Rettig trans.) (Washington, DC: The Catholic University of America Press, 1988), pp. 56–57.

We have shown elsewhere how sacramental liturgy is the site
where being and acting place themselves under the paradigm of
realization and effectuality. It is significant that Ambrose of Milan
accordingly inserts between matter and form 'a third that is
called operative, whose task is to effectuate [*tertium . . . quod
operatorium dicitur, cui suppeteret . . . efficere*]'.[49] Being is now
effectuality and effectuation, as though it possessed within itself,
in the words of Gaius Marius Victorinus, 'an intimate operation':
'operating is itself being, at the same time and simply [*ipsum
enim operari esse est, simul et simplex*]'.[50]

10. In late Scholasticism, in whose systematic formulation
Philosophia prima sive ontologia will be conveyed to
modernity, the problem of possibility finds its topical site
in the definition of essence. Essence is what is first conceived of the being or entity (*quod primum de ente con-
cipitur*) and the reality of an entity is simply defined
through its possibility, in other words, insofar as it does
not contain anything excluding its existence (*ens dicitur,
quod existere potest, consequenter cui existentia non repugnant*). This non-repugnance to exist that defines possibility
(*non repugnantia ad existendum, seu existendi possibilitas*)
is an intrinsic characteristic (*quidnam intrinsecum*) of the

49 Ambrose, *Hexameron*, BOOK 1, CHAP. 1, §1.

50 Gaius Marius Victorinus, *Adversus Arium*, BOOK 1, §4. See Giorgio
Agamben, *Opus Dei: An Archaeology of Duty* (Adam Kotsko trans.) (Stanford:
Stanford University Press, 2013), p. 51.

entity.[51] In Baumgarten's pregnant formulation, essence and possibility are identified with one another; essence is the 'collection of the essential determinations in a possible thing, or its internal possibility [*complexus essentialium in possibili, seu possibilitatis eius interna*]'.[52] In the vocabulary of Scholasticism, *realitas*, 'thingness', coincides with its essence and the latter with its possibility.

Existence, from this perspective, simply becomes a *complementum possibilitatis*, the fulfilment or realization of the internal possibilities contained within essence: 'I thus define existence as a complement of possibility.'[53] As the explanations that follow this definition clearly show, existence is conceived here as something that is added to essence to realize its possibility (*quod accedere debeat* [. . .] *ut possibilitas compleatur*) and to 'transfer the entity from the state of possibility to the state of actuality' (*ut ens ex statu possibilitatis in statum actualitatis traducatur*).[54] Realization is inscribed in essence as its most proper possibility.

51 Christian Freiherr von Wolff, *Philosophia prima sive Ontologia* (Frankfurt and Leipzig, 1730), pp. 137, 115.

52 Alexander Gottlieb Baumgarten, *Metaphysica* (Halle, 1739), par. 40, p. 8. English translation: *Metaphysics: A Critical Translation with Kant's Elucidations, Selected Notes and Related Materials* (Courtney D. Fugate and John Hymers eds and trans) (London: Bloomsbury, 2013), p. 108.

53 Wolff, *Philosophia prima sive ontologia*, p. 143.

54 Wolff, *Philosophia prima sive ontologia*, p. 143.

Already in Suárez's *Disputationes metaphysicae*, which,
alongside Leibniz, are the model for Wolff and
Baumgarten's accounts, the real essence of an entity was
defined as that which does not imply in itself any repug-
nance to exist,[55] and which instead contains—in an
expression that Leibniz will take up in his own *inclinatio
ad existendum*—an aptitude for existence (*eius ratio con-
sistit in hoc, quod sit habens essentiam realem, id est non
fictam nec chymericam, sed veram et aptam ad realiter existendum* [then its nature consists in this, that it is something
having a real essence, that is, not a fictitious or chimerical
essence, but one that is true and suited to really existing]—
II, 4, 5).[56] If we can speak, in this sense, of a primacy of
essence and possibility over existence, this does not mean
that the more or less acknowledged aporias implicit in the
split are thereby resolved. If real essence is not in itself
actual, nevertheless, Suárez writes, it cannot be conceived
without a relation to actual existence (*intelligi non potest
sine ordine ad esse et realem entitatem actualem*), such that
'although to be actually does not belong to the essence of a
creature, nevertheless, a relation to being, or an aptitude
for being [*ordo ad esse vel aptitudo essendi*] pertains to its

---

55 Francisco Suárez, *Disputationes metaphysicae*, DISP. 2, SECT. 4, §7.

56 Suárez, *Disputationes metaphysicae*, DISP. 2, SECT. 4, §5; Francisco
Suárez, *Metaphysical Disputation II: On the Essential Concept or Concept
of Being* (Shane Duarte ed. and trans.) (Washington, DC: The Catholic
University of America, 2023), p. 137.

intrinsic and essential concept [*est de intrinseco et essentiali concepту eius*].'[57]

With an obvious circularity that defines the functioning of the ontological machine, essence cannot be defined except through existence, which in turn is nothing but the complement and realization of essence. And when Suárez writes, 'the essence of a thing [*essentia rei*] is that which we conceive to agree with it primarily, and to be first constituted intrinsically in the being of a thing,'[58] it is not clear what *res* means here, and whether the term does not merely betray the fact that one cannot speak of 'essence' and 'existence' without presupposing the 'thing' (the word 'thing'), from whose split they stem.

---

57 Suárez, *Disputationes metaphysicae*, DISP. 2, SECT. 4, §14; Suárez, *Metaphysical Disputation II*, p. 153.

58 Suárez, *Disputationes metaphysicae*, DISP. 2, SECT. 4, §6; Suárez, *Metaphysical Disputation II*, p. 139.

CHAPTER TWO

The Existence of God

1. The ontological argument is the place where the splitting of the 'thing' of thought and, at the same time, the need to heal the fracture it implies, forcefully appear within medieval thought. It interests us not only, or especially, as the attempt to prove the existence of God, but rather because of the modality in which it tries to demonstrate it. This modality was expressed by Leibniz in the formula *admirabilis transitus de potentia ad actum* (marvellous transition from power to act); in other words, the ontological argument intends to prove the existence of God by thinking a possibility that immediately passes over into being. We lose the philosophical import of the argument if we forget—as the authors themselves sometimes do—that possibility is here an ontological and not merely a logical category. When modern scholars object to the argument that it implies an illegitimate slippage from a logical notion of possibility to a real efficacy, it is this ontological nature of modality that remains in the shadows.

When Anselm, against the *insipiens* (fool) of the Psalms (14:1) who 'says in his heart "There is no God"', concedes that when someone intends a phrase they do not necessarily understand that what they intend exists in reality—because 'one thing is understanding that a thing is in the intellect, another that the thing exists [*aliud enim est rem esse in intellectu, aliud intelligere rem esse*][1]—it is the merely logical notion of possibility that he means to sideline. But there is a single case—God, 'that than which we cannot think something greater'—in which the intelligence of the possibility of a thing and that of its reality coincide. If the fool, the *insipiens*, can say that God does not exist, that is because he has not truly grasped what he believes he thought. You can indeed think a thing by thinking solely the word that signifies it (*cum vox eam significans cogitator*) or by thinking, in the word, the thing itself (*cum idipsum quod res est intelligitur*). At the point that one thinks God—that than which there is nothing greater—in this second manner, possibility and reality, *esse in intellectu* and *esse in re*, are necessarily identified with one another. That is, God is the guarantor of the coincidence between the two fragments of ontological difference, essence and existence, possibility and reality, which everywhere lie divided. That is why, as Scholasticism will declare, God is the *Ens realissimum*, which has always already realized itself.

---

1 Anselm of Canterbury, *Fidens quaerens intellectum* (Alexandre Koyré ed.) (Paris: Vrin, 1982), p. 12.

That the ontological argument is grounded on an obligatory passage from the possible thing to the real thing, in which ontological and logical modalities run the risk of being confused with one another, is evident from the exemplification introduced by Anselm to prove the argument's stringency. He evokes the case—a topical paradigm we already encountered in Augustine to explain the passage from power to act via creation—of a painter who,

> when he thinks in advance [*praecogitat*] the painting he is about to make, has in his mind what he has not yet made, even if he does not understand yet that it exists. But as soon as he has painted it [*cum vero iam pinxit*], then he has it in his mind and at the same time he understands that what he has made exists.[2]

Just as Augustine's chest[3] was already real in the mind of its maker, so that its realization was, so to speak, already implicit within it, in the same way the fool who intends in his intellect the proposition 'God is that than which there is nothing greater' cannot, if he truly understands it, but immediately deduce from it the existence of what he has understood. It is evident that for Anselm, unless we artificially separate the word within thought, language, if we truly understand it, necessarily refers to the *res*, to the

2 Anselm, *Fidens quaerens intellectum*, p. 12.
3 See above, p. 50n48.

thing it signifies. If this thing is such as to imply the necessity of its existence—as happens for the word *God* and for it alone, insofar as it signifies that than which we cannot think anything greater—then intending the word means accepting that God exists.

This is the perspective in which we should read the coeval and brilliant pamphlet by Gaunilo of Marmoutiers in defence of the fool (*Liber pro insipiente*). Gaunilo can happily show that, if the painting or the chest are already real in the art of the maker (*in arte artificis*) because they are part of his intelligence, and as such are alive (*arca quae est in arte vita est*), while the chest that is realized outside of him is not alive (*arca quae fit in opera non est vita*), this cannot be the case for a thing 'simply heard or devised' (*excogitatum*)[4]—because here the reality of the thing and its intellection will instead be heterogeneous and mutually non-deducible. Even if it were true that there is something than which we cannot think something greater, this would certainly not be in the intelligence of the one who thinks it in the same way that the painting which has not yet been turned into a work is already alive and present in the art of the painter. Rather, it would be there like a phrase or a name are in the mind of someone who has heard them and tries to imagine their meaning while not knowing it yet.

---

4 Gaunilo of Marmoutiers, *Gaunilonis liber pro insipiente* in Anselme, *Fidens quaerens intellectum*, pp. 58-60.

Gaunilo's originality does not lie so much in the refutation of the passage from possibility in the mind to reality in things—unduly exemplified by Anselm after the model of the maker—but above all in having imagined in his defence of the fool a dimension of language and thought that he calls 'thought of the word alone' (*cogitatio secundum vocem solam*) in which, while a signifying word is thought, one does not necessarily intend the thing that is signified in it (Anselm: *id ipsum quod res est*). We are dealing with a thought that thinks

> not so much the word itself, which is a thing that is somehow true, namely, the sound of the syllables and letters, but the meaning of the heard word; not, however, as it is thought by one who knows what is usually signified with that word [by whom it is thought according to the thing, *secundum rem*—G. A.] but rather as it is thought by one who does not know the meaning, and thinks only according to the movement of the soul which tries to represent to itself the effect of the heard voice and the meaning of the perceived voice.[5]

In such an experience of language, which is that of the fool, but which Gaunilo identifies as the experience of the word as such—somehow suspended between mere sound

---

5 Gaunilo, *Gaunilonis liber pro insipiente* in Anselme, *Fidens quaerens intellectum*, p. 62.

and actual denotation—it is possible to perceive a signifying word (for example, the word 'God'), without having to accept the existence of the thing signified, just like someone who's heard of a legendary island that some call 'lost' (*Perdita*) and is said to be greater in riches and delights than any other island known to men:

> if someone wished to persuade me that this island exists and that this cannot be doubted, I would believe they are joking and I would not know whom to judge stupider, me for believing him, or him, if he thinks he's proven the existence of that island without first having demonstrated that it is in my intelligence as a thing that is truly and indubitably existing, and not only as something false or doubtful.[6]

2. The refutation of the ontological argument that Aquinas develops at the beginning of his *Summa* is not too different from Gaunilo's. Against those who claim that the comprehension of the meaning of God's name implies his existence, he first objects that because we do not have an adequate knowledge of his essence his existence is not known to us as such. In God, essence and existence certainly coincide,

---

6 Gaunilo, *Gaunilonis liber pro insipiente* in Anselme, *Fidens quaerens intellectum*, pp. 64–66.

but it is not at all possible to prove this—as Anselm claims—
based on a definition, because all we have of God are names.

> Yet, granted that everyone understands that by
> this word 'God' is signified something than which
> nothing greater can be thought, nevertheless, it
> does not therefore follow that he understands that
> what the word signifies exists actually, but only
> that it exists in the intellect [*non sequitur Deum
> esse nisi in intellectu*].[7]

In his first systematic work, the *Commentary on the
Sentences*, the refutation is less unequivocal, because
Aquinas admits that the meaning of the name of God is in
itself known and that Anselm's argument should be understood in the sense that 'once God has been understood,
we cannot intend that God exists and at the same time
think that he does not exist' (*postquam intelligimus Deum,
non potest intelligi, quod sit Deus et possit cogitari non esse*).
From this it does not follow, however, that the fool cannot
think that there is no God, 'for he can think that there is
no such thing as that than which a greater cannot be
thought.'[8]

---

7 Thomas Aquinas, *Summa Theologica*, PART 1, QUES. 2, ART. 1, REP. OBJ. 2;
Thomas Aquinas, *Summa Theologica*, VOL. 1 (Fathers of the English
Dominican Province and Daniel J. Sullivan trans.) (Chicago: Encyclopaedia
Britannica, 1923), p. 11.

8 Thomas Aquinas, *Commentary on the Sentences*, BOOK 1, DIST. 3, QUES. 1,
ART. 2, REP. OBJ. 4.

Once again, the validity of the ontological argument depends on the experience of language that underlies it. The oscillation between logical modality and ontological modality that both the advocates of the argument and its critics seem to succumb to corresponds to the split in the 'thing' of language, whose genealogy we have briefly traced. What is at stake for Aquinas is the twofold meaning— existential and copulative—of the verb 'being' in Indo-European languages, on which we'll have occasion to return and of which, after his own fashion, he is perfectly aware:

> 'To be' can mean either of two things. It may mean the act of being [*actum essendi*], or it may mean the composition of a proposition effected by the mind in joining a predicate to a subject. Taking "to be" in the first sense, we cannot understand God's being nor His essence, but only in the second sense.[9]

We can understand the proposition 'God is that than which we cannot think anything greater', in which 'is' has the value of a grammatical copula; but it is not possible to understand with equal certainty the existential proposition 'God is'. Here begins that process of the progressive separation of existence from essence that will lead, beginning with Kant, to their opposition ('being is not a real predicate').

---

9 Aquinas, *Summa Theologica*, PART 1, QUES. 3, ART. 4, REP. OBJ. 2'; *Summa Theologica*, VOL. 1.

3. It is not surprising that Scotus—after Aquinas's refutation—reprises on new bases the ontological argument, repeatedly undertaking an a priori demonstration of divine existence. We will follow here the exposition from Chapter 3 of *De primo principio* (§§44–57), which is replicated almost verbatim in the later *Ordinatio* (BOOK 1, DIST. 2, PART 1, QUES 1–2) without integrally reproducing its painstaking arguments, which articulate themselves into conclusions, demonstrations and corollaries, in keeping with an expositional canon that likely influenced Spinoza. Scotus cautions that his demonstration does not refer to a 'singular unicum according to number' but to a 'quiddity or nature' (the proof of existence therefore does not concern God but divinity) and that it will proceed on the basis of the possible (*de possibili*) and not from the actual (*de actu*), because proofs according to the act are contingent and only concern actual existence, while the former are necessary and also refer to possible or quidditative existence (§§43–45). It is crucial to understand the strategy that guides the demonstration which, starting from a possible being, grounds its necessity by showing it to be uncausable and uneffectible (the first principle is *ineffectibilis*, namely, unrealizable).

The first thesis (or, to the extent that it is demonstrated, *conclusio*) is that it is possible for there to be an effective nature, namely, one that is capable of producing in being

(§44: *aliqua est natura in entibus effectiva*). If there is an effectible nature—which can be posited in being and realized—then there will also be an effective nature, because the former cannot posit itself in being on its own. The second *conclusio* is that there is an absolutely first efficient, which is not effectible but is effective by its own virtue. If it is denied, then it will be realizable by another (*effectibile ab alio*), in which case the previous argument will have to be repeated, thus leading to an infinite regress, which is impossible (*infinitas est impossibile ascendendo*). There exists therefore a first efficient (§46). The third conclusion is that the absolutely first efficient is uncausable because it is unrealizable (*ineffectibile*) and is effective independently of any other being. This is also proved by the fact that if it were causable by virtue of another, we would again have to grant an infinite process, each time going back until we reached an uncausable and uneffectible being.

The fourth and decisive conclusion is that the absolutely first efficient actually exists (*est in actu existens*). Here too the demonstration proceeds on the basis of the possible: if there can exist (*si potest esse*) something whose *ratio* rejects having its being dependent on others (*posse esse ab alio*), then it exists by itself (*a se*). But, as the third conclusion demonstrated, the *ratio* of the first efficient rejects being able to be by virtue of another and yet it is possible (as follows from the first conclusion). Therefore, the absolutely first efficient can exist by itself. At this point, the fifth conclusion can affirm that the uncausable exists necessarily by itself (*incausabile est ex se necesse esse*). It is in fact impossible that by itself (*ex se*) it is not, because only that which is incompossible with itself can not be. But for an uncausable there can be no incompossible, because such an incompossible would be either from itself or from another. If it were from itself then—according to the fourth *conclusio*—it would actually exist and there would at the same time be two incompossibles, which is impossible as they would mutually exclude one another. And if instead it were from another, not even in that case could it stop the uncaused from necessarily existing, because no caused being can have a being that is more vehement and powerful (*vehementius vel potentius*) than uncaused being.

Modern scholars have objected to Scotus' argumentation that it implies a slippage from a logical notion of possibility to an effectively causal one. As we have seen, this objection only partially hits the mark, because possibility for Scotus is both a logical and an ontological category. When he writes that '[c]orresponding with this logical possibility there is a real potency [*huic possibilitati logicae correspondet potentia realis*]',[10] he does not seek to separate them but to

---

10 John Duns Scotus, *Contingency and Freedom: Lectura I 39* (A. Vos Jaczn, H. Veldhuis, A. H. Looman-Graaskamp, E. Dekker and N. W. Den Bok eds and trans) (Dordrecht: Kluwer, 1994), p. 118 (QUES. 1–5, NOTE 51).

show their correspondence. What preoccupies him is that possibility and existence coincide in God, in other words that they fall together and that God therefore is not only uncausable but also unrealizable (*ineffectibilis*), that is to say that he cannot be caused and produced in being. In this sense, the possibility—both logical and real—of a first and uneffectible being converts itself *ipso facto* into his existence.

No less important, however, is defining the strategy wherein such a coincidence is inscribed and in view of which it must at all costs be proven. The coincidence of possibility and existence equally serves to ground their division in creatures (even in an author who, like Scotus, does not consider this a real but only a formal division). This can be understood if we consider the sixth thesis that concludes the proof: 'the necessity of being of itself belongs to only one nature [*uni soli naturae convenit*].'[11] We are not interested here in the arguments through which Scotus demonstrates the coincidence, but with the consequence that he leaves unuttered: if there is only one being in which possibility and existence coincide then in all other entities they can be divided. Conversely, if possibility and existence are divided in creatures then there must be one being— and only one—in which they coincide. The machinery of

---

11 John Duns Scotus, *The De Primo Principio of John Duns Scotus* (Evan Roche trans.) (St Bonaventure, NY: The Franciscan Institute, 1949), p. 53 (§57).

the ontological argument serves to provide both the coincidence and the separation of possibility and reality. Because there is an unrealizable, everything else is realizable—vice versa, if everything is realizable then there must be an unrealizable.

4. The ontological argument reappears unexpectedly in Descartes. Like Aquinas, he objects to Anselm that the latter's argument is grounded only in the comprehension of a name and the sole consequence that can be legitimately drawn from it is that '*when we understand what the word God means, we understand that it means that God exists effectively as well as in the mind*: but because a word signifies something, that is no reason for this being true.'[12] The argument that Descartes advances refers instead not to the comprehension of a name but to that of 'the true and immutable nature of anything, its essence, or form,'[13] and 'everything I clearly and distinctly perceive to belong to the thing does in fact belong to it [*revera ad illam pertinere*]'.[14] And since God is the absolutely perfect being (*Ens*

---

12 René Descartes, 'Reply to Objections I' in *The Philosophical Works of Descartes*, VOL. 2 (Elizabeth S. Haldane and G. R. T. Ross trans) (New York: Dover, 1934), p. 19 [translation modified].

13 Descartes, 'Reply to Objections I', p. 19.

14 René Descartes, *Meditations on First Philosophy* (Michael Moriarty trans.) (Oxford: Oxford University Press, 2008), p. 47.

perfectissimum) it follows that its existence belongs to its nature with the same necessity whereby the fact that the sum of the angles of a triangle is equal to two right angles belongs to the nature of the triangle.

It has been noted that Descartes is playing here on the meaning of the term 'thing', which seems to designate an essence or idea as well as an object existing outside the mind. And it has been objected to his proof that it implies a fallacious passage from a logical possibility to a real possibility, and moreover that because he was indeed aware of the weakness of his argument, in the *First Replies* to the objections levied against him he develops a new form of the argument in which God is presented as *causa sui*. Yet Descartes cautions that this concept is not to be understood in a solely negative way, in the sense that there is no cause to God's existence, but also positively, in the sense that the power of God is such that he has always already brought himself into existence:

> when we say that God exists *per se*, we can indeed understand that negatively, our whole meaning being really that He has no cause. But, if we have previously enquired why He is or why He continues in being, and having regard to the immense and incomprehensible power which exists in the idea of Him we recognize that it is so exceedingly

great that it is clearly the cause of His continuing
to be, and that there can be nothing else besides
it, we say that God exists per se, no longer
negatively but in the highest positive sense [...]
we cannot feign that anything exists *per se* as to
which no reason can be given regarding why it
exists rather than does not exist; hence there is no
reason for not interpreting self-originated in the
sense in which it implies causal power, that power,
to wit, which passes all bounds.[15]

The fact is that with Descartes the Scholastic concept of
realitas, which coincided with essence and quiddity, under-
goes a transformation that shifts it decisively towards existence. In his analysis of the concept of reality in the
Meditations, Jean-Christophe Bardout has accordingly
written that in Descartes 'reality is no longer a form or
element belonging to essence but turns, so to speak,
towards existence.'[16] It is important not to miss that this
veritable 'existentialization of reality'[17] is produced because,
starting from the third *Meditation*, the notion of *realitas* is
intimately tied to that of cause. Descartes repeatedly affirms
that the reality of the effect derives from its cause and that

---

15 Descartes, 'Reply to Objections I', pp. 15–17.

16 Jean-Christophe Bardout, 'Note sur les significations cartésiennes de la
réalité', *Quaestio* 17 (2017): 186.

17 Bardout, 'Note sur les significations cartésiennes de la réalité': 195.

it's evident that 'there must be at least as much reality in the total and efficient cause as in its effect. For, I ask, from where could the effect derive its reality [*assumere realitatem*], if not from the cause?'[18] As Bardout suggests, 'reality is treated as an existent, precisely to the extent in which it is now made to depend on the efficiency of its cause.'[19] This means that Descartes, developing insights that we already encountered in Scotus, conceives reality and existence as the result of a process of effectuation—that is, not as a reality but as a realization (this is why he can also render reality by the term *perfectio*). And it is this conception—no less significant than his doctrine of the subject—that Descartes has bequeathed to modern philosophy.

From this point of view, the true novelty of the Cartesian argument, which wrests it from the circularity it would otherwise collapse back into, is that it is grounded in the experience of a power or possibility that exceeds any logical deduction. As Descartes writes,

> the light of nature certainly tells us that nothing exists about which the question, why it exists, cannot be asked. [...] But I frankly allow that something may exist in which there is such a great and inexhaustible power [*tanta et tam inexhausta*

18 Descartes, *Meditations*, p. 29.
19 Bardout, 'Note sur les significations cartésiennes de la réalité': 187.

potentia—the French version renders this as *une puissance si grande et si inépuisable*—G. A.] that it has needed no assistance in order to exist [. . .] such a cause I understand God to be.[20]

Descartes returns several times to this idea of a surplus or overabundant divine power, in which possibility is no longer a simple concept but harbours within itself a veritable force, a *vis existendi*. What 'has from itself the force to exist [*vim per se existendi*] [. . .] undoubtedly has the force to possess in reality all the perfections of which it has the idea in itself, that is, all the perfections I conceive to be in God.'[21]

5. The Cartesian idea of possibility as power and *vis existendi* is picked up, albeit with some divergences, both by Spinoza and Leibniz. Spinoza's *Ethics* opens with a definition that already contains within itself the ontological argument: 'By cause of itself [*causa sui*] I understand that whose essence involves existence, *or* that whose nature cannot be conceived except as existing.'[22] Proposition VII of Part I

---

20 Descartes, 'Reply to Objections I', p. 14.

21 Descartes, *Meditations*, p. 36 [translation modified].

22 Baruch Spinoza, *The Ethics* in *The Spinoza Reader: The Ethics and Other Works* (Edwin Curley trans. and ed.) (Princeton, NJ: Princeton University Press, 1994), p. 85.

coherently states the proof in these terms: *Ad naturam substantiae pertinet existere*, which the demonstration summarily proves: 'A substance cannot be produced by anything else [. . .] therefore it will be the cause of itself, that is [. . .] its essence necessarily involves existence, *or* it pertains to its nature to exist'.[23]

It has been objected to this demonstration—and the first to do so was Leibniz himself—that it transformed a logical inference into a causal inference. This means not understanding that Spinoza starts precisely from Descartes' *causa sui* and his *vis existendi*. This is already evident in his first work, in which he expounds the *Principles of Cartesian Philosophy*. Here, commenting on a passage in Descartes in which the power to conserve oneself is at stake, Spinoza already discretely formulates in a note what will become the fundamental principle of his thought, namely, that 'the force by which a substance is conserved is nothing outside its essence and differs from it only in name'.[24] In the Appendix, to which the note refers, we thus read that 'God's power is not distinct from his essence,'[25] and we are told that the divine essence is nothing other than the force

23 Spinoza, *Ethics*, p. 88.

24 Baruch Spinoza, *Principles of Cartesian Philosophy* (Harry E. Wedeck trans.) (London: Peter Owen Ltd, 1961), p. 36.

25 Spinoza, 'Appendix: Thoughts on Metaphysics', PART 2, CHAP. 3 in *Principles of Cartesian Philosophy*, p. 153.

through which God perseveres in his being, in other words his life:

> We therefore understand by *life the power through which things persist in their being*. And, since that power is different from the things themselves, we rightly say that these things have life. But the power by which God persists in His being is merely His essence. Hence they make a very acceptable assertion when they say that God is life.[26]

In Proposition 7 of the third part of the *Ethics* he will call this force *conatus*: 'The tension [*conatus*, the customary translation as 'striving' is imprecise—G. A.] by which each thing strives to persevere in its being is nothing but the actual essence of the thing.'[27] In any case, in the demonstration of Prop. 7 of the *Principles*, the decisive element is indeed the *vis se ipsum conservandi*, and Spinoza can state the ontological argument in the form: 'Whoever has the power to conserve himself, has a nature involving necessary existence,' following this by, 'Whoever has the power of self-conservation [. . .] needs no external cause in order to exist, his nature alone being a sufficient cause for his existence, either possibly or necessarily.'[28]

---

26 Spinoza, Appendix, PART 2, CHAP. 6 in *Principles of Cartesian Philosophy*, p. 161.

27 Spinoza, *Ethics*, p. 159 [translation modified].

28 Spinoza, *Principles of Cartesian Philosophy*, p. 39.

In the scholium to Prop. 11 of the first part of the *Ethics*, in which the argument is stated anew, the demonstration of the existence of God is founded on the power or force he has to exist:

> For since being able to exist is power, it follows that the more reality belongs to the nature of a thing, the more powers it has, of itself, to exist. Therefore, an absolutely infinite Being, *or* God, has, of himself, an absolutely infinite power of existing. For that reason, he exists absolutely.[29]

This is why Spinoza separates power from simple possibility as a modal category; while power coincides with the actual essence of each thing and with the conatus of persevering in its being, simple possibility, which he also calls contingency, only expresses a defect of our knowledge:

> For if we do not know that the thing's essence involves a contradiction, or if we do know very well that its essence does not involve a contradiction, and nevertheless can affirm nothing certainly about its existence, because the order of causes is hidden from us, it can never seem to us either necessary or impossible. So we call it contingent or possible.[30]

---

29 Spinoza, *Ethics*, p. 92.

30 Spinoza, *Ethics*, p. 107 (PART 1, PROP. 33, SCH. 1).

What is at stake in Spinoza's ontological argument is not possibility as a modal category but an actual power or force, and there can be properly speaking no passage from power to act because power is already real and does not need to realize itself. It is the lack of cognizance of this decisive point, among those philosophers who insist on seeking a passage between the two planes of being, which produces the continual slippage from a logical-modal plane to an ontological power and vice versa, which so often leads to contradictions in the arguments of these authors as well as their interpreters.

6. Leibniz's critique of Descartes' argument remains within a logical-modal conception of the proof. It is a matter, once again, of finding that *admirabilis transitus de potentia ad actum* which all have sought without ever really attaining it. Ignoring the *vis existendi* so forcefully evoked by Descartes and Spinoza, Leibniz maintains in fact that their argument is fallacious because it can only work if we pre-suppose that God is possible. As he writes in a letter from 3 January 1678 to Hermann Conring: 'I have discovered that from their argumentations it is evinced that God exists necessarily, only if we suppose that he is possible.' Descartes tried and failed he adds, 'either to prove with a sophism

this possibility of divine existence or to free himself from the obligation of proving it.'[31]

Leibniz offers two different corrections of the Cartesian argument. The first, which he says he's shown 'to Mister Spinoza' (*Domini Spinosae*) while in The Hague, consists in proving that all the perfections are compatible, namely, that they can all be in the same subject. 'There can thus be a subject of all the perfections, namely, the absolutely perfect Being. Therefore it is evident that the latter exists, since existence is contained in the number of perfections.'

In the 1701 text *De la démonstration cartésienne de l'existence du Dieu du R. P. Lami*, Leibniz instead reformulates the proof as follows: *Si l'être necessaire est possible, alors il existe* (If necessary being is possible, then it exists). The argument's stringency stems from the fact that necessary being and being-existing-by-its-own-essence are the same thing. To deny that being-by-itself is possible means negating every possibility:

> *Car si l'être de soi est impossible, tous les êtres par autrui le sont aussi; puis qu'ils ne sont enfin que par l'être de soi; ainsi rien ne sçauroit exister. Ce raisonnement nous conduit à une autre importante proposition modale, égale à la précédente, et qui,*

---

31 Gottfried Wilhelm Leibniz, *Die philosophischen Schitften von Gottfried Wilhelm Leibniz* (Carl Immanuel Gerhardt ed.) (Berlin: Weidmannsche Buchhandlung, 1878–90), VOL. 1, p. 188.

jointe avec elle, achève la demonstration. On la pourrait énoncer ainsi: si l'être necessaire n'est point, il n'y a point d'être possible. Il semble que cette demonstration n'avoit pas été portée si loin jusqu'ici.[32]

For if being by itself is impossible, all beings by another are impossible too; because in the end they are only by virtue of being by itself; thus, nothing could exist. This reasoning leads us to another important modal proposition, equal to the foregoing and which, together with it, completes the demonstration. It can be stated as follows: if necessary being is not, there can be no possible being. It seems that this demonstration had not been taken so far until now.

It is striking that, while resorting to an argument grounded in the *causa sui*, Leibniz does not evoke the theme, present both in Descartes and Spinoza, of power as *vis existendi*. Even more remarkable in that one of the most original feats of his philosophical genius is precisely a new theory of possibility, in which, as has been noted, he appears to extend to every essence the logic of the ontological argument.[33] This theory finds its decisive formulation in the

32 Leibniz, *Die philosophischen Schitften von Gottfried Wilhelm Leibniz*, VOL. 4, pp. 405–6.

33 Arthur O. Lovejoy, *The Great Chain of Being: A Study of the History of an Idea*, new EDN (New Brunswick, NJ, and London: Transaction Publishers, 2009[1936]), p. 166.

theorem according to which *omne possibile exigit existere* (everything possible demands to exist). Possibility ceases to be a merely logical category and constitutively contains within itself an exigency or inclination to exist. As we read in *De veritatibus primis*: '*nisi in ipsa essentiae natura quaedam ad existendum inclinatio esset, nihil existeret* [unless there were in the very nature of essence an inclination to exist, nothing would exist]'. Leibniz accordingly distinguishes between the 'bare power' conceived by the Scholastics, which 'needs an external excitation and almost a stimulus to be transferred into act' and power as 'active force' which, if there are no impediments, actualizes itself and can be compared to 'a suspended weight that stretches the cord that holds it aloft or to a stretched bow.'[34] In another text, to express this propension to exist of every possible, he forges, on the basis of the future infinitive of the verb *existere*, the term *existiturentia*. The reason why something exists, he writes, 'lies in the prevalence of the reasons to exist over those to not exist, or if I can express it in one word, in the *existiturentia essentiae*, in the urge to exist of essence [...] from this it follows that every possible tends by itself towards existence.'[35] This exigency or urge towards existence is not a being of reason but something that exists objectively:

---

34 Leibniz, *Die philosophischen Schitften von Gottfried Wilhelm Leibniz*, VOL. 4, p. 471.

35 Gottfried Wilhelm Leibniz, *De ratione cur haec existant potius quam alia* in *Sämtliche Schriften und Briefe*, Philosophische Schriften, VOL. 6 (Heinrich Schepers ed.) (Berlin: Akademie Verlag, 1990), p. 1634.

of the *existiturentia* of essence there must be a root existing in things [*a parte rei*], otherwise in essence there would be nothing but an artifice devoid of reality [*animi figmentum*], and since nothing can be produced from nothing, it would follow that there would be nothing but a perpetual and necessary nothing.[36]

To bridge the split between possible and real, possibility must in turn divide into a bare power (whose reality is inert and cannot translate by itself into act) and a force that is always tending—like a bow about to shoot an arrow—towards its own realization. The ontological argument therefore evolves—even if this seems to escape the awareness of its authors—from an *a priori* logical deduction to the idea that a *vis existendi*, an inclination towards the act, operates within possibility. But in this way the problem of the passage from the possible to the real further complicates itself.

It should be clear at this juncture why we have said that in the ontological argument philosophy seeks to recompose that splitting of the thing of thought into essence and existence, possibility and reality, which it had itself produced. Nowhere does this attempt manifest its contradictoriness as much as in the stubbornly pursued idea of an *admirabilis*

---

36 Leibniz, *De ratione cur haec existant potius quam alia*, p. 1635.

transitus de potentia ad actum. In fact, there is no passage since possibility is itself real and already contains within itself the force that makes it exist; and yet, with the sole exception of Spinoza, who transforms the *vis existendi* into a *conatus* internal to substance, philosophers continue to seek this impossible Northwest passage in the ocean of metaphysics. The split in the thing of thought and language is not something that philosophy can tackle without putting that very split into question.

7. In modern thought, it is in Kant that the problem of the thing and of its twofold, antinomic reality—possible and actual—is most strikingly manifest. This will lead him to sunder the concept of reality at the level of terminology, distinguishing the *Realität* of what is simply possible from *Wirklichkeit*, effective existence. But it will also compel him to resurrect, albeit critically, the ancient Platonic name of the idea (*to pragma auto*, 'the thing itself'), in order to give the name 'thing in itself' (*Ding an sich*) to the most problematic theme of metaphysics.

It is not by chance then that Kant feels the need to tackle the ontological argument, namely, the site at which the fracture of reality was put back together, the site of its re-composition. In Kant's refutation, the ambiguity of the thing and its reality is already manifest in the theorem that constitutes the argument's core: 'Existence is obviously not a real predicate' (*Sein ist offenbar kein reales Prädicat*), where *reales* does not mean 'existing' but, in keeping with the logic of late Scholasticism, refers to the affirmation of a thing or essence as possible. In the first refutation of the argument, Kant's 1763 text 'The Only Possible Argument in Support of a Demonstration of the Existence of God'— in which the theorem took the form: 'Existence [*Dasein*] is not a predicate or a determination of a thing [*von irgend einem Dinge*]'[37]—the ambiguity lies in the term 'thing,' which can mean both a possible and an existent.

If we follow Kant's reasoning in the 1763 text, we see that it rests on the strict separation of existence from the set of predicates of a thing.

> If I say: 'God is omnipotent' all that is being thought is the logical relation between God and omnipotence, for the latter is a characteristic mark of the former. Nothing further is being posited here. Whether God is, that is to say, whether God is posited absolutely or exists, is not contained in the original assertion at all.[38]

When God instead pronounces his *fiat* on a possible world,

37 Immanuel Kant, 'The Only Possible Argument in Support of a Demonstration of the Existence of God (1763)' in *Theoretical Philosophy, 1755-1770* (David Walford with Ralf Meerbote eds and trans) (Cambridge: Cambridge University Press, 1992), p. 117.

38 Kant, 'Only Possible Argument in Support of a Demonstration of the Existence of God', p. 119.

He does not grant any new determinations to the whole which is represented in His understanding. He adds [*setzt . . . hinzu*] no new predicate to it. Rather, He posits [*setzt*] the series of things [. . .] The relations of predicates to their subjects never designate anything existent; if they did, the subject would then have to be already posited as existent.[39]

To the question 'if in existence there is more than in simple possibility', Kant can thus reply that we must distinguish between 'what is posited' (*Was da gesetzt sei*) and 'how it is posited' (*wie es gesetzt sei*) (this is the classic Scholastic distinction between *quidditas*, 'what thing a thing is,' and *quodditas*, 'the fact that it exists'). With a reasoning whose subtlety he himself perceives (*in einer so subtilen Vorstellung*), he can conclude that

nothing more is posited in an existent thing [*in einem Existierenden*] than is posited in a merely possible thing [. . .] But more is posited through an existent thing [*durch etwas Existierendes*] than is posited through a merely possible thing, for positing through an existent thing involves the absolute positing of the thing itself as well [*auf absolute Position der Sache selbst*].[40]

39 Kant, 'Only Possible Argument in Support of a Demonstration of the Existence of God', p. 120.

40 Kant, 'Only Possible Argument in Support of a Demonstration of the Existence of God', p. 121.

That is why Kant criticizes as 'imprecise' (*unbestimmt*) the Wolffian definition of existence, according to which for something to exist something must be added to possibility through which the possible receives its fulfilment (*Erfüllung*), which is what we call reality (*Wirklichkeit*). Existence is not a complement or fulfilment of the possible but is entirely heterogeneous to all this. Similarly, Crusius' affirmation according to which the where (*irgendwo*) and when (*irgendwen*) would be 'unmissable determinations' of existence is rejected by showing that these also belong to a merely possible thing: 'Without doubt, the eternal Jew, Ahasuerus, is, in respect of all the countries through which he is to wander and all the times through which he is to live, a possible person.'[41] Existence is thought by Kant as so heterogeneous to mere predicates that not even spatial and temporal determinations constitutively belong to it.

Though there is no passage between the possible and the existent, Kant nonetheless retains here a logical relation between them, without which the ontological apparatus could not function: 'if all existence is cancelled, then nothing is posited absolutely, nothing at all is given, there is no material element for anything which can be thought; all possibility completely disappears.'[42] In effect, there is

---

41 Kant, 'Only Possible Argument in Support of a Demonstration of the Existence of God', p. 122.

42 Kant, 'Only Possible Argument in Support of a Demonstration of the Existence of God', p. 123.

no contradiction in the negation of all existence, but 'to say that there is a possibility and yet nothing real at all is self-contradictory. For if nothing exists, then nothing which could be thought is given either, and we contradict ourselves if we still wish to say that something is possible.'[43]

That existence is not a real predicate was already somehow implicit in Scotus' thesis according to which existence is not distinguished from essence like one *res* is distinguished from another but is nothing other than the ultimate *realitas* of essence. Even Gassendi, in his objection to Descartes, appears to deny that existence could be conceived as a property or predicate of a thing: 'Whether you consider existence in God or in any other subject, it is by no means a perfection, but only a form, or an act without which perfection could not be.'[44] The thesis is formulated in an even more radical guise by Pierre Desmaizeaux: 'I utterly deny that existence is a perfection. In effect, I cannot persuade

---

43 Kant, 'Only Possible Argument in Support of a Demonstration of the Existence of God', pp. 123–24.

44 The original 1641 Latin edition of the *Meditations*, and translations from it, do not feature references to 'form' or 'act' in this sentence. The classic Italian translation by Adriano Tilgher was based on the 1647 French translation by Duc de Luynes with Claude Clerselier (responsible for rendering Gassendi's objections). The passage in French reads: '*Mais à vray dire, soit que vous consideriez l'existence en Dieu, soit que vous la consideriez en quelqu'autre sujet, elle n'est point une perfection, mais seulement une forme, ou un acte sans lequel il n'y en peut avoir*'. René Descartes, *Les méditations métaphysiques* (Paris: The widow of Jean Camusat and Pierre Le Petit, 1647), p. 499.

myself that it adds anything to the nature of a thing. Whether a being exists or does not exist does not make its essence either more or less perfect in my view.'[45] In his reply to Gassendi, Descartes instead appears convinced that existence is a property of the thing: 'Here I cannot see what kind of thing you think existence is, or why you think it cannot be called a property.'[46] Philosophers seem here to divide into those who consider existence to be a property of the thing and those who do not.

8. In the *Critique of Pure Reason*, Kant tackles the ontological argument once again and provides a new and more precise refutation of it. While the problem of the relationship between language and thought is never thematized as such, and he could not be aware that he was thereby defining a specific characteristic of Indo-European languages, Kant dwells on the clear distinction between the two meanings of the 'little word "is"' (*das Wörtchen: ist*)—the predicative (the copula of the grammarians), in which the concept is put in relation with another, and the existential, in which the existence of a thing is affirmed.

> The judgement God is omnipotent contains two concepts that have their objects: God and omnipotence; the little word 'is' is not yet a predicate in

45 Pierre Desmaizeaux, 'Article II. Lettre de Mr. Des Maizeaux à l'Auteur de ces Nouvelles', *Nouvelles de la republique des lettres* (November 1701): 510–19; here, p. 514.

46 Descartes, *Meditations on First Philosophy*, p. 196.

it, but only that which posits the predicate in relation to the subject. Now if I take the subject (God)
together with all his predicates (among which
omnipotence belongs), and say God is, or there is
a God [*Gott ist oder es ist ein Gott*], then I add no
new predicate to the concept of God, but only
posit the subject in itself with all its predicates,
and indeed posit the object in relation to my concept. Both must contain exactly the same, and
hence when I think this object as given absolutely
[*schlechtin gegeben*] (through the expression, 'it
is'), nothing is thereby added to the concept, which
expresses merely its possibility. Thus the real [*das
Wirkliche*] contains nothing more than the merely
possible.[47]

Here Kant introduces the notorious example of the hundred
thalers, which was to elicit the ironic criticisms of Hegel,
Feuerbach and Marx:

A hundred actual thalers do not contain the least
bit more than a hundred possible ones. For since
the latter signifies the concept and the former its
object and its positing in itself, then, in case the
former contained more than the latter, my concept
would not express the entire object and thus would

---

47 Immanuel Kant, *Critique of Pure Reason* (Paul Guyer and Allen W. Wood
trans. and ed.) (Cambridge: Cambridge University Press, 1998), p. 567 (A
599/B 627) [translation modified].

not be the suitable concept of it. But in my financial
condition there is more with a hundred actual
thalers than with the mere concept of them (that
is, their possibility). For with actuality the object
is not merely included in my concept analytically,
but adds [*kommt . . . hinzu*] synthetically to my
concept [. . .] yet the hundred thalers themselves
that I am thinking of are not in the least increased
through this being outside my concept. Thus when
I think a thing, through whichever and however
many predicates I like (even in its thoroughgoing
determination), not the least bit gets added
[*kommt . . . hinzu*] to the thing when I posit in
addition that this thing is. [. . .] Thus whatever
and however much our concept of an object may
contain, we have to go out beyond it [*aus ihm
herausgehen*] in order to provide it with existence.[48]

9. Consider the peculiarity of the Kantian operation. He
takes a 'thing' (God or one hundred thalers—but the
examples are surely not random) and splits its reality into
possibility (which corresponds to the analytical predicative
affirmation: 'God is omnipotent') and existence (which
corresponds to the synthetic thesis: 'God is'). We could

48 Kant, *Critique of Pure Reason*, pp. 567–68 [translation modified].

say, in this regard, that he is unwittingly making it possible to think the double structure of the verb 'to be' so as to affirm its radical heterogeneity. Between the predicative and the existential [*esistentivo*][49] meanings, between the hundred possible thalers and the hundred real thalers there is no passage. Kant's thesis is in perfect agreement with that of a modern linguist like Émile Benveniste, when the latter observes that 'there is no connection, either by nature or by necessity, between the verbal notion of "to exist, to be really there" and the function of the "copula", and that the creation of a verb 'to be' in order to express the predicative relation between two terms 'was not inscribed in any linguistic destiny',[50] as proven by its absence in many languages, like Arabic and Hebrew.

The fact is that the division as well as the promiscuity between the two meanings of the verb 'to be' is at the basis of Western ontology and of the split between essence and existence, possibility and reality, which defines it. One and the same *res*, one and the same reality splits depending on whether we consider it in its 'what' (the *quid est*, the *quidditas* or essence of the ontological tradition) or in its pure

---

49 *Esistentivo*, as opposed to *esistenziale*, is the Italian translation of Heidegger's *existenziell*, rendered as 'existentiell' by the first English-language translators of *Sein und Zeit*. See Martin Heidegger, *Being and Time* (John Macquarrie and Edward Robinson eds) (Oxford: Blackwell, 1962), p. 33. [Trans.]

50 Émile Benveniste, *Problems in General Linguistics* (Mary Elizabeth Meek trans.) (Coral Gables, FL: University of Miami Press, 1971), p. 164.

existence (the *quod est* or *quia*, that this thing be). This is why Kant can say that the two realities, considered according to essence or possibility, have the same predicative content and yet, as regards their existence, are absolutely heterogeneous—in other words, that I have to exit both possibility and the mere concept to reach existence.

That the problem of the relationship between possibility and reality nonetheless remains problematic in Kant is made manifest by the meticulousness with which he tries to underscore its difference when the time comes to define modal categories. Both reality and possibility belong in effect to this class of categories which, according to Kant, 'have this peculiarity: as a determination of the object they do not augment the concept to which they are ascribed in the least, but rather express only the relation to the faculty of cognition.'[51] The only difference between them is that an object is said to be possible when it agrees (*überein-kommt*) with the formal conditions of experience, and is instead said to be real (*wirklich*) when it is connected (*zusammenhängt*) with the material conditions of experience, that is to say with a perception. In both cases we are thus dealing with a certain relation to the faculty of cognition and not with a property of the thing.

---

51 Kant, *Critique of Pure Reason*, p. 322 (A 219/B 266).

THE EXISTENCE OF GOD · 93

The possibility and reality that Kant is concerned with are always solely referred to possible experience for a subject and are never a determination of the thing itself. That is why Kant can write, multiplying terminological subtleties, that modal categories are synthetic only in a subjective sense, inasmuch as 'they add to the concept of a thing (the real [*realen*]), about which they do not otherwise say anything, the cognitive power whence it arises and has its seat.'[52] Kant feels compelled to add a note here that details with similar subtlety that

> [t]hrough [*durch*] the actuality [*Wirklichkeit*] of a thing I certainly posit more than possibility, but not in the thing [*in dem Dinge*]; for that can never contain more in actuality than what was contained in its complete possibility. But while possibility was merely a positing of a thing in relation to the understanding (to its empirical use), actuality is at the same time its connection with perception.[53]

Terminological cautions notwithstanding, not only can the fundamental split of the *res* that governs Western thought not be eliminated, but every possibility of repairing it falls away. The doubling of the possible and the real which, as modal categories, limit themselves to putting objects in relation with the faculty of cognition and 'do not say

---

52 Kant, *Critique of Pure Reason*, p. 332 (A 234/B 286).

53 Kant, *Critique of Pure Reason*, p. 333 (A 235/B 287).

anything' about the thing, refers back to another more decisive partition, in which we can speak about the thing only on condition of placing it beyond our faculty of cognition. As Kant unreservedly affirms in the Introduction to the second edition of the *Critique*, our cognition 'reaches appearances [*Erscheinungen*] only, leaving the thing in itself as something actual [*wirklich*] for itself but uncognized by us'.[54] In this sense, Kant can say that the thing in itself puts a limit on possible experience. True reality, just like true possibility, is situated in the unknowable, namely, beyond that which appears: 'if we cannot cognize these same objects as things in themselves, we at least must be able to think them as things in themselves. For otherwise there would follow the absurd proposition [*der ungereimte Satz*] that there is an appearance [*Erscheinung*] without anything that appears [*erscheint*]'.[55] The thing thereby splits into thing (*Ding*) as object of experience and thing in itself (*Ding an sich*), of which there is no experience. The *res* in its truth has slipped into the impossible. It is a pure noumenon, the transcendental object = x.

54 Kant, *Critique of Pure Reason*, p. 112 (B xx).

55 Kant, *Critique of Pure Reason*, p. 115 (B xxvi).

10. In the history of Western philosophy, Kant represents the moment in which the break between the thing and thought is revealed as irreparable. What is at stake in the Kantian critique of the ontological argument and in his doctrine of modality is therefore the definitive crisis of that *admirabilis transitus* from the possible to the real that philosophy had not stopped chasing after, because upon it was founded what we have called the ontological machine of the West. Kant drains possibility of its *vis existendi* and thus strips it of all reality. Metaphysics is now impossible, except in a peculiar form, namely, as empty space or inevitable illusion. Possibility and reality are categories of modality, which only express the relation of an object with the faculty of cognition and say nothing about the object as such; moreover, there can be no *vis existendi* in essence and possibility, because existence is not a real predicate, and it is radically heterogeneous to both essence and possibility. As Gilson has written, in Kant 'the two orders of the real and the possible are incommensurable.'[56]

Philosophical tradition and grammatical reflection have so accustomed us to taking this break for granted that we are not aware that it constitutes the aporetic core of the *dispositif* on which, from the very start, ontology grounded its specific power. Essence and existence, power and act,

---

56 Étienne Gilson, *L'Être et l'essence*, 3rd EDN (Paris: Vrin, 2000), p. 10.

possibility and reality are the two faces or two parts of the ontological machine of the West. Ontology is not in fact an abstruse excogitation unrelated to reality and history; it is, on the contrary, the place in which epochal decisions pregnant with consequences are taken. Without the splitting of reality (of the 'thing' of men) into essence and existence, and into possibility (*dynamis*) and actuality (*energeia*), neither scientific knowledge nor the capacity to control and durably guide human actions that characterizes the historical power of the West would have been possible. If we were not able to suspend the exclusive concentration of our attention on what exists immediately (as animals seem to do), to think and define its essence (the 'what'), Western science and technology would have certainly not experienced the development that characterizes them. And if the dimension of possibility were to disappear completely, neither plans nor projects would be thinkable and human actions could not be either directed or controlled. The incomparable power of the West has in the ontological machine one of its essential presuppositions.

But the split on which the machine bases its prestige is anything but unproblematic. For the machine to function, the two parts it has separated must be newly articulated with one another, so that their harmonious conflict or discordant consonance may constitute its secret motor. If possibility and reality, essence and existence were absolutely separate and non-communicating, knowledge and action would lose their object while thought and things, language and the world, would remain unrelated. This means that the passage between essence and existence, and between possibility and reality, constitutes the decisive problem of Western metaphysics, on which it never ceases to be ship-wrecked; but it also means that an exit from metaphysics is not possible without a critique of the split in the thing and of the paradigm of realization which that split implies.

In quantum physics, the merely statistical consistency of reality implies that reality cannot be known in itself deterministically, but that it must always be realized in an experiment. No reality in itself is given as such: it is nothing but the 'realization' of a probability and this realization can only take place through the intervention of the researcher. The true meaning of Heisenberg's indeterminacy principle is not so much that of placing a limit on knowledge, but that of legitimating as inevitable the inter-vention of the experimenter. As Ettore Majorana put it: 'The result of any measurement seems therefore to concern the state that the system is placed in during the course of the experiment rather than the unknowable one in which it found itself before being perturbed.'[57] We can then understand why Simone Weil could affirm that with quantum physics the West had unsus-pectingly 'lost science, or at least the thing that had been called

---

57 Ettore Majorana, 'Il valore delle leggi statistiche nella fisica e nelle scienze sociali' (1934) in *Che cos'è reale?* (Giorgio Agamben ed.) (Vicenza: Neri Pozza, 2016), p. 76.

by that name for the last four centuries.'[58] What has been lost is in truth the correct conception of possibility and reality. Just as, for theologians, the existence of God cannot be experienced in itself, but, in the ontological argument, is 'realized'—thereby allowing it to pass from the possible to the real—so in quantum physics reality is not in itself accessible but the researcher 'realizes' its probability each and every time by way of experiment.

11. In our brief genealogy of the splitting of the *res* in the history of philosophy, we have encountered several times the problem of language which, in medieval and modern philosophers up to Kant, often appears without ever being explicitly thematized—or so it looks. This is true especially for the double meaning (copulative-grammatical and existential [*esistentivo*]-lexical) of the verb 'to be' in classical languages, which, as Benveniste has shown, does not correspond to any inherent necessity and about which medieval theologians seem to be somehow aware. Benveniste himself, in a famous essay,[59] demonstrated that the Aristotelian categories that have so forcefully determined philosophical reflection really correspond to the structural categories of the Greek language. The table of the ten categories that

58 Simone Weil, 'Classical Science and After' in *On Science, Necessity, and the Love of God* (Richard Ress ed. and trans.) (Oxford: Oxford University Press, 1968), p. 3.

59 Benveniste, 'Categories of Thought and Language' in *Problems in General Linguistics*, pp. 55–64.

Aristotle elaborated and bequeathed to Western philosophy as the framework of the general and permanent conditions of thought is nothing but the conceptual projection of a given linguistic situation. In particular, the first category—*ousia* or substance—corresponds to the linguistic class of names (something that ancient grammarians had already noticed, when they defined 'substantive' names—*nomen substantivum*—precisely in relation to Aristotelian substance). The division between essence and existence, which Benveniste does not mention, could therefore also correspond—besides to the two meanings of the verb 'to be' in Greek and Latin—to the lexical distinction between the name that designates an individual (the first *ousiai*, which Aristotle exemplifies with a proper name or with 'a certain man' or 'a certain horse') and the name as general category (animal, man).

The distinction between essence and existence, possibility and reality could also have been influenced by another structural partition in the languages familiar to us, on which Benveniste insisted in his final investigations, namely, the one between the level of names (the lexicon) and the level of discourse (in Benveniste's terms, the difference between the semiotic—language as a system of signs—and the semantic—language as an actual discourse). This is a difference that Greek philosophers—at least ever since Heraclitus (Fragment 1) and Antisthenes—were perfectly aware of. Plato states it limpidly in the *Theaetetus*:

the primary elements, as it were, of which we and
everything else are composed, have no account.
Each of them, in itself, can only be named; it is not
possible to say anything else of it [. . .] it is impossible that any of the primaries should be expressed
in an account; it can only be named, for a name is
all that it has [*onoma gar monon echein*].[60]

And he adds in the *Protagoras* that 'underlying each of
these names is a particular existence [*ousia*]'.[61] (Proposition
3.221 of Wittgenstein's *Tractatus*, upon closer inspection,
does not say anything different: 'Objects can only be *named*.
[. . .] I can only speak *about* them: I cannot *put them into
words*.')[62]

The distinction between essence (power) and existence
(act) corresponds perfectly to the one between name and
discourse, between language as a system of signs and language as an actual discourse. In this sense, we could say
that it does nothing but articulate a structure implicit in
language, and that we could accordingly wonder whether
thought's advance is not unwittingly determined, as
Benveniste suggests, by the language it uses. Every time
we reflect on the influence that linguistic categories wield

---

60 Plato, *Theaetetus* (M. J. Levett and Myles Burnyeat trans) in *Complete Works*, p. 223 (201e–202b).

61 Plato, *Protagoras* (Stanley Lombardo and Karen Bell trans) in *Complete Works*, p. 779 (349b) [translation modified].

62 Ludwig Wittgenstein, *Tractatus Logico-Philosophicus* (D. F. Pears and B. F. McGuinness trans) (London: Routledge, 2001), p. 15.

over the categories of thought, we must not forget that the influence is often reciprocal. The structure of language at a given moment of its historical unfolding is not, in effect, a natural given; it is determined at least in part by philosophical and grammatical reflection, that is by the process whereby speaking beings become aware of what they are doing when they speak. The awareness of using a language is, in other words, inseparable from the patient labour of analysis and construction that results in the creation of that language's grammatical identity. Benveniste thus showed that the copulative meaning of the verb 'to be' in Greek was originally lacking and was replaced by the nominal phrase, which unites two words in a syntagm devoid of a verb (*ariston ydor*, which today we translate: 'the best thing is water'). It is likely the philosophical and grammatical reflection on language that has led us to conceive the nominal phrase as a phrase that implies the verb 'to be', thereby determining its gradual decline and replacement (albeit not in every case) with the phrase with the copula 'is', which becomes the normal expression. The primacy, beginning with Aristotelian logic, of apophantic judgement (in the form subject-verb-predicate) over other forms of discourse has been no stranger to this process. Similarly, we are so accustomed to considering the partition between names and discourse as a fundamental structure of language that we are unaware that the isolation of something like a name (which in Indo-European languages presents itself in a plurality of inflected forms that differ from one another—the so-called cases) is no doubt the result of a slow process, whose outcome the ancients deemed so important as to attribute its discovery to Plato and Aristotle. The systematic articulation of the difference between semiotic and semantic in modern linguistics is so far from being a natural given that Benveniste was finally forced to admit that, from the point of view of linguistics, between the two levels there is no passage, and that if in order to speak we truly had to move from the level of names to that of the phrase, from potential language to actual discourse, the instance of the word would be impossible.

If the aphasia that struck the great linguist shortly after having penned this paradoxical diagnosis prevents us from knowing how he might have tried to come to terms with it, it is certainly instructive to try to situate in this perspective the split between essence and existence and between possibility and reality, whose abridged archaeology we have traced in these pages. In other words, it can be seen as an answer, as deep as it is problematic, to the question: 'What does it mean to speak, what are we doing when we speak (when we think)?' We continuously pass from the level of the interpretation of the world that confronts us with the pure being-there of things (the plane of names or existence) to the effort to comprehend 'what' defines them and makes them be what they are (the plane of discourse or essence); and, inversely and just as incessantly, from this second plane to the first, depending on whether the dominant model is essence (possibility) or existence (actual reality). The 'thing' that language has revealed to us is always already split, and, what's more, this very splitting allows us to know and dominate the things of the world that we constantly come up against.

To bring into question this conception that has determined the philosophy of the West for so long will thus mean to try to think the experience and cognition of the world otherwise than through an improbable splitting and a no less improbable passage between possibility and reality and between essence and existence; and just as decidedly, to try to think the experience of language otherwise than as an unattainable passage from the level of names to that of propositions. It is certain, in any case, that neither can the structure of language on its own permit a comprehensive account of the articulation of thought, nor can thought unfold in full autonomy from the language in which it is expressed. It is possible, instead, that true philosophy consists in a clinch [*corpo a corpo*] or rather, a ceaseless *synousia* [intercourse] between thought and language, in which neither of the two contestants—or comrades—can ever claim to have definitively mastered the reasons and conditions that the other imposes upon and proposes to it.

It's enough to consider our sources with greater care to appreciate that the link between the ontological problem and the experience of language had not escaped the philosophers. Even if we leave aside the awareness of it that Plato and Aristotle could have had (Plato, in *Cratylus*, emphatically asks 'if the primary names are indeed names, they must make the things that are as clear as possible to us. But how can they do this when they aren't based on other names?'[63] while Aristotle continually repeats that 'being is said'), medieval philosophers knew with sufficient clarity the link between the meaning of names and the ontological difference. As Albertus Magnus writes:

> Two things must be observed in names, that is the form or reason through which they are imposed [*forma sive ratio a qua imponitur*] and what they are imposed on [*illud cui imponitur*]: and these are called by some meaning and supposit [*significatum et suppositum*] and by grammarians quality and substance [*qualitas et substantia*].[64]

Analogously, in Peter Helias' *Summa super Priscianum* (twelfth century), a text that lucidly thematizes the relation between philosophical and grammatical analysis, we can read that

> every name signifies the 'what' [*quod est*] and 'that through which' [*id quo est*], like the name 'man' signifies

---

63 Plato, *Cratylus* (C. D. C. Reeve trans.) in *Complete Works*, p. 139 (422d).

64 Albertus Magnus, *Commentarii in Sententiarum*, BOOK 1, DIST. 2, ART. 1, SOL. in *Opera omnia*, VOL. 25 (Auguste Borgnet ed.) (Paris: 1893), p. 55.

what it is, namely, the thing that is a man [*rem quae est homo*] and that through which it is, namely, the humanity through which it is man, because man is such on the basis of humanity.[65]

65 Quoted in Lambertus Marie de Rijk, *Logica modernorum: A Contribution to the History of Early Terminist Logic, Volume 2: Part One, The Origin and Early Development of the Theory of Supposition* (Assen: Van Gorcum & Company, 1967), p. 231.

CHAPTER THREE

The Possible Is the Real

1. It should be clear at this point in what sense we can now unreservedly state the thesis that the ontological-political machine of the West is grounded on the splitting of being into possibility and reality. This splitting of being has its origin in Aristotle. In the *Categories*, he distinguishes the singular existent, which he calls *ousia prote* ('first substance') and can only be designated with a proper name or deictic (Socrates, this man, this horse), from second substances and from all other forms of being, which are said only on condition that the first substance is presupposed. As he writes:

> All the other things are either said on the presupposition [*cath'hypokeimenou*, literally 'on the lying under'—G. A.] of the primary *ousiai* or are on the presupposition of them [. . .] For example, 'animal' is predicated of man and therefore also of this particular man; for were it predicated of no particular

man it would not be predicated of man in general. [. . .] So if the primary substances did not exist it would be impossible for any of the other things to exist; everything else, in fact, is said on the presupposition of their lying under or is in this presupposition.[1]

The primacy of primary substances is reiterated a few lines further: 'primary substances [*ousiai*], to the extent that they lie under [*hypocheistai*] all the other things and all the other things are predicated of them or are in them, are called *ousiai* most of all'.[2] It is important to note that by defining the *ousiai* as 'primary', Aristotle implicitly introduces into them a temporal anteriority. As he will say unconditionally in the *Metaphysics* (1028a30), that which lies at the basis and on which the secondary substances are predicated precedes them not just logically but also according to time (*kai logoi kai gnosei kai chronoi*).

It is on account of the primacy of this sub-jective deter-mination of being as first *hypokeimenon*, as non-predicable singularity that lies-under-and-at-the-basis of every linguistic predication, that in the tradition of Western philosophy the term *ousia* is translated in Latin by *substantia*. Beginning with neo-Platonism, in effect, the treatise on

---

1 Aristotle, *Categories* in *Categories and De Interpretatione* (J. L. Ackrill trans.) (Oxford: Clarendon Press, 1963), p. 6 (2a34–2b6) [translation modified].

2 Aristotle, *Categories*, p. 7 (2b15–17) [translation modified].

the *Categories* takes on a privileged position in the corpus of Aristotle's works and, in its Latin translation, exercises a determining influence on medieval culture. Boethius, in whose version the Middle Ages came to know the *Categories*, though recognizing that the more correct translation would have been *essentia*,[3] employed instead the term *substantia*, thereby orienting in a decisive way the vocabulary and understanding of Western ontology. Being can appear as that which lies-under-and-at-the-basis only from the point of view of linguistic predication, namely, on the grounds of that primacy of the subjective determination of *ousia* as proper name and first *hypokeimenon* that stands at the centre of Aristotle's *Categories*. The entire lexicon of Western ontology (*substantia, subiectum, hypostasis, subsistentia*) is the result of this primacy of first substance as lying at the bottom of every predication.

In the seventh book of the *Metaphysics*, however, Aristotle seems to put into question the primacy of what lies at the basis and to affirm instead its insufficiency, in order to replace it with another determination of *ousia* that he calls *to ti en einai* ('the what it was to be'—in medieval translations, *quod quid erat esse*). What we need to understand is

---

3 *Ousia* is a deverbal noun formed on the basis of the participle of the verb *einai*, and in his theological treatise against Eutyches and Nestorius, Boethius therefore makes the term *essentia* correspond to *ousia*, reserving *substantia* for the Greek *hypostasis*.

the meaning of this apparent contradiction in Aristotelian thought and in the strategy that is at stake within it. The determination of *ousia* as *hypokeimenon*, lying-at-the-bottom, is—and this is how Aristotle argues for his turn—insufficient and obscure (*adelon*) and furthermore risks being confused with the determination of matter (*hyle*), which in the *Physics* Aristotle had defined as the first *hypokeimenon* subtending any change. The *sub-iectum*, that which lies under every predication can, in effect, only be named and indicated; it enters into propositions only as that of which something is said and predicated. In this sense, notwithstanding its immediate evidence, it remains *adelon*, not manifest. The consequence—as Rudolph Boehm demonstrated in an exemplary study—is a fundamental split between being and discourse: on the one hand, a first lying-at-the-bottom, of which everything is said and predicated, but which itself remains unsayable and unpredicable; on the other, everything that is said about it or which is in it. Or, on one side an existent that is, so to speak, inessential, the pure fact that something is there, without the 'what it is' (as the medievals would say: a pure *quod est* without a *quid est*); on the other, an inexistent essence: 'Essence and existence each fall outside the other, in the double meaning of the term: they break with the other and they break apart.'[4]

---

4 Rudolph Boehm, *Das Grundlegende und das Wesentliche* (The Hague: Martinus Nijhoff, 1965), p. 169.

It is with the aim of repairing this split, of thinking the unity of existential [*esistentivo*] being and predicative being, that Aristotle introduces the *ti en einai*, which literally stands for 'what it was (for that certain being, for example Socrates) to be (Socrates)'. What is decisive, as has been shown, is the introduction in this formula of a verb in the past tense: *en*, not simply 'what it is' but 'what it was'. If the first sub-ject was pre-supposed as what lies at the foundation of every discourse, it can be grasped in its truth only as a past, only through time. The individual, as first substance, can be defined and not simply named only by grasping its existence in the past, only by introducing time into being. That is to say, according to the new formulation of *ousia*, by trying to understand 'what it was for Socrates— for that certain sub-ject—to be Socrates'. Essence is nothing but existence pushed back into the past and—only in this way—grasped.

It is this temporal regression that will lead to the equation of existence with the act, and of essence with possibility or power. In the *Metaphysics*, Aristotle defines power (*dynamis*) and act (*energeia*) as 'two ways in which being is said' and repeatedly insists on the priority of the act (*energeia*) over power (*dynamis*). He begins by identifying the act with 'the existence of the thing' (*to yparchein to pragma*) (*Metaphysics* 1048a36) and, forgoing a definition of power's way of being, he affirms that we must make do with understanding it by analogy: the act is to power 'as the process of building is related to the ability to build; as waking is to sleeping; as seeing is to closed eyes; as what has been moulded out of a material is to the material; as what has been shaped is to the unshaped.'[5] Shortly before, he evokes the example of the statue, 'we say that something is potentially like Hermes is in the wood.'[6] He thereby surreptitiously shifts the two categories from the ontological sphere to that of human techniques and of action. If we can say that the statue of Hermes is potentially in the wood, this is because we have seen somewhere a wooden statue of Hermes and possibility is thus nothing but a pre-supposition of existence; however, in the course of his argument, having to explain what defines human techniques—for instance, the activity proper to the architect or to the zither player—he seems to think something like a transit or passage from power to act. Thus, in the *De anima* he employs the expression 'leading one who thinks or understands into actuality from potentiality [*eis entelecheian agein ek dynamei ontos*]',[7] though we should note that he never uses terms like 'passage' or 'transit', but simply writes 'becomes', as in 'he who potentially has science becomes an actual knower [*theoroun ginetai ton echon ten epistemen*]'.[8]

---

5 Aristotle, *Metaphysics* (Richard Hope trans.) (Ann Arbor: University of Michigan Press, 1960), p. 188 (1048b1–5).

6 Aristotle, *Metaphysics*, p. 188 (1048a30–33).

7 Aristotle, *De Anima* (Christopher Shields trans.) (Oxford: Clarendon Press, 2016), p. 33 (417b10).

8 Aristotle, *De Anima*, p. 33 (417b5).

In Book Theta of the *Metaphysics*, Aristotle does not tire of repeating that '*energeia* is anterior [*proteron*] to possibility-power', according to discourse (*toi logoi*) and existence (*tei ousiai*) as well as according to time (*chronoi*). What is particularly instructive, however, is the restriction that he introduces at this point with regard to temporal anteriority: if we consider power and act with regard to species, the act precedes possibility (a man is generated by another man and reality precedes possibility); but if we consider them with respect to the single individual then possibility is anterior (the seed precedes the individual and the possible precedes the real). It is just this circularity that shows the constitutive link between possibility and temporality; if, as Aristotle did with *ousia*, we introduce time into being, then the latter will split into power and act, possibility and reality, and only through their partition will it be comprehended. Possibility and reality will be distinct but also inseparable: just as it is not true to say that something is possible if it will never exist (*Metaphysics* 1047b3), it is equally absurd to argue that someone can be defined as an architect without ever having built or a zither player without having ever played that instrument (1049b30–32). And yet it is precisely the split between power and act that makes it possible to understand what it means to be an architect or a zither player. What we call the possible is nothing but a projection of the real into the past, just as essence is nothing but a pre-supposition of existence; but in both cases what is at stake in the division is the effort to understand being through time, to grasp its reality as a process of derealization and realization. To grasp the act and existence, we must shift them as possibilities into the past; but this possibility or power must then in some way be newly translated into existence and act.

This is what Bergson lucidly shows in the essay 'The Possible and the Real', published in Swedish in 1930, to 'express my regret at being unable to go to Stockholm to give a lecture, as was the custom, on the occasion of the bestowal of the Nobel prize.'[9] He declares that he wishes above all to question 'the idea that the possible is *less than* the real, and that, for this reason, the possibility of things precedes their existence.'[10] If we attentively consider the concrete reality of life and consciousness, we notice, in effect, that in the possible there is more and not less than in the real: 'For the possible is only the real with the addition of an act of mind which throws its image back into the past, once it has been enacted.'[11] Bergson reprises the Aristotelian example of the artwork (the Hermes statue), transposing it to the ambit of literature and the dramatic arts. To believe that Hamlet pre-existed in Shakespeare's mind means unduly transferring the purely negative idea of possibility, in the sense of that which is not impossible, into that of the pre-existence of the idea in the mind

9 Henri Bergson, 'The Possible and the Real' in *Key Writings* (Keith Ansell Pearson and John Mullarkey eds) (London: Continuum, 2002), p. 382n2.

10 Bergson, 'The Possible and the Real', p. 228.

11 Bergson, 'The Possible and the Real', p. 232.

of the author. What really happens is that a man of genius creates a work: 'it will then be real, and by that very fact it becomes retrospectively or retroactively possible. It would not be possible, it would not have been so, if this man had not come upon the scene.'[12] The temporal status of the possible is really the future anterior: regarding the work, we should say that it 'will have been' possible, once the artist has produced it.[13]

Responding to the objection that in this manner the present seems to introduce something into the past, Bergson says that what is thereby inserted into the past is not something real, but rather the possible.

> As reality is created as something unforeseeable and new, its image is reflected behind it into the indefinite past; thus it finds that it has from all time been possible, but it is at this precise moment that it begins to have been always possible, and that is why I said that its possibility, which does not precede its reality, will have preceded it once the reality has appeared. The possible is therefore the mirage of the present in the past [. . .] Thus in judging that the possible does not presuppose the real, one admits that the realization adds something to the simple possibility: the possible would have been there from all time, a phantom awaiting its hour; it would therefore have become reality by the addition of something, by some transfusion of blood or life. One does not see that the contrary is the case, that the possible implies the corresponding reality with, moreover, something added, since the possible is the combined

---

12 Bergson, 'The Possible and the Real', p. 229.
13 Bergson, 'The Possible and the Real', p. 229.

effect of reality once it has appeared and of a condition which throws it back in time. The idea immanent in most philosophies and natural to the human mind, of possibles which would be realized by an acquisition of existence, is therefore pure illusion.[14]

With this analysis of the logical *dispositif* of possibility, Bergson drastically disproves the mirage of a transit from possibility to existence which had nourished the speculations of philosophers about the ontological argument. Power and act are generated together, they are co-originary, and the error lies not so much in distinguishing them, as in thinking that power pre-exists separately and that the problem is that of defining the way in which the passage from power to act is articulated.

2. In a decisive passage from *De monarchia*, Dante, while referring back to Averroes [Ibn Rushd], thinks possibility and its relation to the act in an original manner, all of whose consequences we need to ponder. First, he inscribes power or possibility in the very definition of human nature and the 'purpose of human society as a whole' (*finis totius humanae civilitatis*).[15] Seeking the specific property of *humana universitas* with respect to the other creatures, he identifies it not in the intellectual faculty simply understood, but in the possibility or power of thinking:

---

14 Bergson, 'The Possible and the Real', pp. 229–30.

15 Dante Alighieri, *Monarchy* (Prue Shaw trans. and ed.) (Cambridge: Cambridge University Press, 1996), p. 5 (BOOK 1, CHAP. 3).

the highest faculty in a human being is not [. . .] to exist as a living thing, for plants too share in that; nor is it to exist as a creature with sense perception, for that is also shared by the lower animals; but it is to exist as a creature who apprehends by means of the potential intellect: this mode of existence belongs to no creature (whether higher or lower) other than human beings. For while there are indeed other beings who like us are endowed with intellect, nonetheless their intellect is not 'potential' in the way that man's is, since such beings exist only as intelligences and nothing else, and their very being is simply the act of understanding that their own nature exists; and they are engaged in this ceaselessly [*sine interpolatione*], otherwise they would not be eternal. It is thus clear that the highest potentiality of mankind is his intellectual potentiality or faculty.[16]

Recovering an Averroist theme, Dante here defines the proper nature of humanity not by the uninterrupted act of thought, but by the possibility or power of thinking. While angelic nature is defined by thinking *sine interpolatione*, without interruption, to human intelligence there belongs a discontinuity that constitutes it as 'power to think', or, according to the terminology of the Averroist tradition, 'possible intellect'.

16 Dante, *Monarchy*, pp. 6–7.

Yet this power is not something like a separate substance or a faculty that precedes the act of thought; it is simply an *interpolatio*, a discontinuity and an alteration (the Latin term can also carry a negative connotation) of the act. The thinking subject inscribes itself, in other words, into the act of intellection as an interpolation in the technical sense: both an alteration and a 'possibility' of thinking. That is why Dante immediately adds:

> And since that potentiality cannot be fully actualized all at once [*tota simul in actu reduci non potest*] in any one individual or in any one of the particular social groupings enumerated above, there must needs be a vast number of individual people in the human race, through whom the whole of this potentiality can be actualized; just as there must be a great variety of things which can be generated so that the whole potentiality of prime matter can continuously be actualized [*sub actu*]; otherwise one would be postulating a potentiality existing separately from actualization, which is impossible.[17]

It is worth pausing on the expression *sub actu*, which signifies an extreme proximity or even coincidence, as in *sub luce* (as day breaks) or *sub die* (within the same day). This technical formula can be found in authors whom Dante knew (like Siger, who writes that matter *semper est sub actu*

---

17 Dante, *Monarchy*, pp. 6–7.

aliquo [is always in some act]),[18] or whom he could have known, such as Berthold of Moosburg or Giles of Rome. Particularly significant in the latter is a passage from his *In Secundum Librum Sententiarum Quaestiones* in which it is clear that power is not a reality separate from the act:

> The active [intellect] does not make power into power [. . .] nor does it make the act into the act, because this pertains to the act as such; for the act to be the act no operation is required [*non indiget aliqua factione*]. What the active [intellect] does is to make the act be potentially and to make power [*potentia*] be in the act [*sub actu*].[19]

It is the action of the active intellect that produces in the act a discontinuity and a power (a 'possible intellect' in the Averroist sense), which cannot, however, be separated from it, but remains constantly *sub actu* (in the case of humankind, thanks to *multitude*).

From this perspective, it is entirely misguided to speak, like Leibniz and the tradition we have examined, of a transit or passage from power to act. What happens is rather the opposite and, in terms that should by now be familiar, what we should say is not that 'every possible demands to

---

18 Siger de Brabant, *Quaestiones in tertium de anima* (Bernardo Carlos Bazán ed.) (Louvain and Paris: Publications Universitaires, 1972), p. 30.

19 Giles of Rome, *In Secundum Librum Sententiarum Quaestiones*, PART 1 (Venice: Zilletus, 1581), DIST. 3, QUES. 1, ART. 2 (p. 171).

exist' but that 'every existent demands its possibility, it demands to become possible'. Possibility or power is certainly real, but not like something that precedes the act and must perfect itself within it, but as a discontinuity and an interpolation of the act that is integral to it and can never be separated from it. That is why Dante diverges from Averroes, who had separated the possible intellect from the soul ('he would separate / *possible intellect* from soul', *'fé disgiunto dall'anima / il possibile intelletto'*):[20] power and act, possibility and reality, are inseparable parts of human intelligence, they define its life and inmost movement ('so that one single soul is formed complete, / that lives and feels and contemplates itself', *'e fassi un'alma sola / che vive e sente e sé in sé rigira'*[21])

In Dante, the power of thought does not just define the specific power of *humana civilitas*, it also lies at the foundation of the experience of love. It is not possible to grasp the poetics of the *stil novo* if we do not first understand that the theory of love it implies reprises and develops the Averroist doctrine of the union of the single individual with the active intellect. Beatrice and the other feminine figures whom the poets celebrate as objects of love name the phantasms of the imagination which, according

---

20 Dante Alighieri, *The Divine Comedy, Volume 2: Purgatory* (Mark Musa trans.) (London: Penguin, 1985), canto 25, lines 64–65, p. 271.

21 Dante, *Purgatory*, canto 25, lines 74–75, p. 271.

to Averroes, guarantee the union (tellingly defined as *copulatio* or *continuatio*) of individuals with the active intellect. As we have tried to demonstrate elsewhere,[22] the brilliant invention of Dante and Guido Cavalcanti is to have situated the experience of love in the possible intellect—that is to say, in the experience of a power and not an act, of an interpolation and not a stable possession. The subject in love—which coincides with this interpolation as well as with the poeticizing subject—experiences in the death of the beloved image the amorous conjunction with the active intellect.

3. A conception of power as immediately coinciding with the act and of possibility as existing absolutely is advanced by Nicholas of Cusa in the trialogue that bears the significant title *De possest*. What is at stake is thinking afresh that unity of power and act which as we saw defines the divinity in the theological tradition. At the same time, it is a matter of defining the problematic identity between God and all things that the apostle Paul had unreservedly affirmed (*ut sit deus omnia in omnibus*, 'that God may be all in all', 1 Corinthians 15:28).

Nicholas starts from the thesis according to which 'every creature that actually exists can simply be' (*omnis enim creatura actu existens utique esse potest*)[23] and develops

---

22 Giorgio Agamben and Jean-Baptiste Brenet, *Intellect d'amour* (Lagrasse: Verdier, 2018).

23 Nicholas of Cusa, *Trialogus De Possest* (Paris: Vrin, 2006), p. 26.

it through a series of logically connected paradoxes. The absolute power of every entity to be what it actually is coincides with

> the absolute actuality through which everything that actually is is what it is [...] From the moment that actuality actually exists, all the more can it be, for an impossible being is not [*cum igitur actualitas sit in act, utique et ipsa esse potest, cum impossibile esse non sit*]. Nor can absolute possibility itself be other than power [*a posse*], just as absolute actuality cannot be other than the act. And that which we have called possibility cannot precede actuality, in the sense that we say that some power precedes the act. How could it ever proceed to the act [*prodisset in actum*], if not through actuality? If the possibility of being [*posse fieri*] were produced by its own accord in the act, it would already be actual before it became actual. Therefore, the absolute possibility that we are discussing, through which the things that actually exist can actually be, neither precedes nor follows actuality. How could actuality exist if possibility did not exist? Absolute power, the act and their nexus are therefore co-eternal.[24]

---

24 Nicholas, *Trialogus De Possest*, p. 28. ['Actually' here and in subsequent quotes from Nicholas translates the Italian *in atto*. −Trans.]

It is on the basis of this identity between power and act in God that Pauline pantheism can be correctly thought.

> If [. . .] God is absolute power, the act and their nexus and is therefore actually every possible being, it is evident that He is all things in the mode of implication [*patet ipsum complicite esse omnia*]. All things, in fact, which in some way exist or can be, are implicated in the first principle and all things that have been or will be created, are explicated by Him in whom they are implicated [*explicantur ab ipso in quo complicite sunt*].[25]

To explain this implication of all things in the absolute power of God, Nicholas resorts to the concept of 'not other [*non aliud*]', which he had defined in the homonymous treatise.[26] God is all things in the sense that He cannot be other than them, that He is not-other than them. The coincidence between absolute possibility and absolute actuality results in the impossibility of being other than all the things that are. Divine omnipotence is defined solely through this singular limitation (*Deus ergo est omnia, ut non possit esse aliud. Ita est undique, ut non possit esse alibi* [Therefore God is everything, so that He is not able to be anything else. He is everywhere, so that He is not able to

---

25 Nicholas, *Trialogus De Possest*, p. 30.

26 See Jasper Hopkins, *Nicholas of Cusa on God as Not-other: A Translation and an Appraisal of 'De Li Non Aliud'* (Minneapolis: University of Minnesota Press, 1979). [Trans.]

be elsewhere]).[27] Insofar as he is capable of everything that he is [*può tutto ciò che è*], God is not so much identical to things, as 'not-other' to them.

This is why the most proper name of God is, according to the neologism that Nicholas coins at this juncture, *Possest*, 'can-is' [*poter-è*]—that is, an absolutely existent power:

> Let us look for an expression that signifies in an extremely simple formula the complex meaning 'power is' [*posse est*]. And since what exists is actually, to be able to be [*poter essere*] is nothing other than to be able to be actually. Let us call it, if you will, *possest*. Everything is implicated in it and it is a sufficiently suitable name for God according to the concept than man has of Him.[28]

From this definition of God as a power to be [*poter essere*] that exists absolutely and actually is everything that can be, there derive further paradoxes. Such a power to be coincides in God with the absolute first principle:

> I understand that you affirm that this name *possest*, composed of *posse* and *esse*, has a simple meaning, which according to the human concept enigmatically leads the enquirer to a positive assertion about God. You understand absolute power insofar as it complicates every power beyond action and

27 Nicholas, *Trialogus De Possest*, p. 38.

28 Nicholas, *Trialogus De Possest*, p. 40.

> passion, beyond being able to make [*poter fare*] and being able to become [*poter diventare*]. And I understand that that this power is actually [*in atto*]. This being which you say is actually all that can be [*tutto il poter essere*] is the absolute. What you thereby mean to say is that where all power actually is, there we attain the first omnipotent principle.[29]

At this point, one of the three speakers in the dialogue suggests that this possibility that eternally exists in the principle is something akin to an uncreated and always already existent matter. Even if the others reject this idea, it is clear that Nicholas could not have overlooked the analogy between his primordial absolute power [*potenza*] and the eternal matter of classical thought.

To think a possibility that is capable of everything that it is means thinking within each and every thing the unity of power, act and their nexus (or, as Nicholas suggests in a floral image, the triune nature of the potential rose, the actual rose and the rose in power and act), while at the same time attaining the principle of all things, namely, the trinity that in God is absolutely in the beginning. That is why the dialogue can move towards its conclusion through a meditation on the preposition 'in'. Absolute power is nothing but an 'in', a being *in* the principle as *in* all things:

---

29 Nicholas, *Trialogus De Possest*, p. 58.

I now consider how through IN one enters into God and into all things. Everything that can be named does not contain in itself anything other than IN. If in fact IN did not exist, all things would count for nothing and would be totally empty. Thus, when I look into substance [*in substantia*], I see the same IN substantiated; if I look into the sky [*in caelum*], I see it celestified; and if in a place, I see it placed.[30]

To think an absolute power that coincides with the act means thinking only a 'being in': the power in the act, the act in the power, and their nexus as a being that is non-substantial but, as it were, purely prepositional: an absolute 'in', simple and perfect.

In the same IN there is first the I then the N and their nexus, so that there is a single word IN, composed of the I, the N and their connection. Nothing is simpler than the I [. . .] The N is generated first, translating into itself the extremely simple I [. . .] In the IN, the I is explicated [. . .] Since the IN, which fills all things and without which they would be empty, inheres in and is immanent to [*inest et immanent*] them, integrating and informing them, it is the first perfection of each and every thing.[31]

---

30 Nicholas, *Trialogus De Possest*, p. 86.

31 Nicholas, *Trialogus De Possest*, p. 86.

If possibility is liberated in this way by Nicholas from every subjection to existence and, at the same time, insofar as it is already perfect in itself, from the necessity of actualization [*di passare all'atto*], the limit of the trialogue is that the problem of potentiality [*potenza*] is continually led back to its theological locus. In other words, Nicholas thinks—no doubt in a more original way—that same coincidence in God of power and act, essence and existence, which the ontological argument had stubbornly sought to define.

4. The Heideggerian reopening of the problem of being in *Sein und Zeit* implies a radical rethinking of the category of possibility. If already in the second chapter of the Introduction, apropos of phenomenology, we find the lapidary thesis according to which 'higher than actuality [*Wirklichkeit*] stands *possibility*,'[32] in the subsequent chapters the latter ceases to be a modal category alongside others and instead defines the very structure of the being that Heidegger calls 'being-there' (*Dasein*). Understanding, as 'a basic mode of Dasein's *Being*,'[33] is above all a power-to-be (*Sein-können*).

---

32 Heidegger, *Being and Time*, p. 63.
33 Heidegger, *Being and Time*, p. 182.

Dasein is not something present-at-hand [*Vorhandenes*] which possesses its competence for something by way of an extra; it is primarily Being-possible [*ein Möglichsein*]. Dasein is in every case what it can be, and in the way in which it is its possibility. [...] The Being-possible which Dasein is existentially in every case, is to be sharply distinguished both from empty logical possibility and from the contingency of something present-at-hand, so far as with the present-at-hand this or that can 'come to pass.' As a modal category of presence-at-hand, possibility signifies what is *not yet* actual [*Wirklich*] and what is *not at any time* necessary. It characterizes the *merely* possible. Ontologically it is on a lower level than actuality and necessity. On the other hand, possibility as an *existentiale* is the most primordial and ultimate positive way in which Dasein is characterized onto-logically.[34]

Dasein does not face possibilities that it can indifferently choose or abandon, but rather, like Nicholas' *possest*, it itself exists in the mode of a power-to-be and is nothing other than this power-to-be:

---

34 Heidegger, *Being and Time*, p. 183.

In every case Dasein, as emotively situated in its own being, has already got itself into definite possibilities. As the potentiality-for-Being which it *is*, it has let such possibilities pass by; it is constantly waiving the possibilities of its Being, or else it seizes upon them and makes mistakes. But this means that Dasein is Being-possible which has been delivered over to itself [*ihm selbst überantwortetes Möglichsein*]—thrown possibility through and through. Dasein is the possibility of Being-free for its ownmost potentiality-for-Being.[35]

Insofar as it is delivered over to its own power-to-be, Dasein does not make projects, it is not free to choose this or that possibility, but it is always already thrown into the project (*Entwurf*) in its ownmost structure, in the sense that project and possibility define its 'existential-ontological Constitution,'[36] and not some faculties that it could avail itself of.

It is therefore not surprising that, when it comes to defining the ownmost possibility of Dasein as being-towards-death, this possibility shows that it has no content other than impossibility; in other words, than its being

---

35 Heidegger, *Being and Time*, p. 183 [translation modified]. [The passage begins: 'Possibility, as an *existentiale*, does not signify a free-floating potentiality-for-Being in the sense of the "liberty of indifference" (*libertas indifferentiae*).']

36 Heidegger, *Being and Time*, p. 177.

THE POSSIBLE IS THE REAL · 129

constitutively unrealizable. "'Being towards" a possibility—
that is to say, towards something possible—may signify
"Being out for" something possible, as in concerning ourselves with its realization [*Verwirklichung*]. Such possibilities are constantly encountered in the field of what is
ready-to-hand and present-at-hand—what is attainable,
controllable, practicable, and the like.'[37] On the contrary,
being-towards-death as its specific possibility cannot offer
to Dasein anything to realize.

> For one thing, death as possible is not something
> possible which is ready-to-hand or present-at-
> hand, but a possibility of *Dasein's* Being. So to
> concern oneself with actualizing what is thus poss-
> ible would have to signify suicide. But if this were
> done, Dasein would deprive itself of the very
> ground for an existing Being-towards-death.[38]

The fact is that one's ownmost possibility coincides with
the possibility of an impossibility.

> Death, as possibility, gives Dasein nothing to be
> 'realized', nothing which Dasein, as real, could
> itself *be*. It is the possibility of the impossibility of
> every way of comporting oneself towards anything,
> of every way of existing. In the anticipation of this
> possibility it becomes 'greater and greater'; that is

---

37 Heidegger, *Being and Time*, p. 305 [translation modified].

38 Heidegger, *Being and Time*, p. 305 [translation modified].

to say, the possibility reveals itself to be such that it knows no measure at all, no more or less, but signifies the possibility of the measureless impossibility of existence [*die Möglichkeit der masslosen Unmöglichkeit der Existenz*].[39]

At this point, Heidegger's strategy becomes clear: in trying to withdraw it from the purview of modality, he flattens possibility onto another modal category, impossibility, and thereby turns the impossible into the only content of Dasein's ownmost possibility. As has been noted, this means reversing the principle of Wolffian ontology according to which from the impossible only the impossible follows: the impossible is here instead the originary source of possibility and the aforementioned thesis needs to be complemented by the codicil according to which '*higher than possibility stands impossibility*'.[40] Yet the novelty with regard to the ontological tradition is less radical than it may seem. If possibility is here unrealizable, this is not because it is real in itself, but rather because its content is impossible. As a structure constitutive of Dasein, it does not have to realize itself in the act, but this simply means that Dasein, which has to be the power-to-be [*poter essere*] in which it is thrown, does not properly have anything to be. To make possible a possible being [*potere un poter essere*] is, as such, impossible.

---

39 Heidegger, *Being and Time*, p. 307.

40 Costantino Esposito, 'L'impossibilità come trascendentale: Per una storia del concetto di impossibile da Suárez a Heidegger', *Archivio di filosofia* 78(1) (2010): 310.

We can now understand why the ultimate structure and sense of Dasein can be nothing other than temporality.[41] The connection with Aristotelian ontology, in which the difference between essence and existence implicated time ('the being that was'), here becomes particularly evident. If temporality is the 'being outside of oneself, the *ekstatikon* pure and simple', Dasein, which has to be its own impossible power-to-be, is accordingly always already ecstatically in time. However, the possibility that times reveals to it is null:

> The primordial and authentic future is the 'towards-oneself' [*Auf-sich-zu*] (to *oneself*), existing as the possibility of nullity, the possibility which is not to be outstripped. The ecstatical character of the primordial future lies precisely in the fact that the future closes one's potentiality-for-Being; that is to say, the future itself is closed to one [*geschlossen*], and as such it makes possible the de-cided [*entschlossene*] existentiell understanding of nullity. Primordial and authentic coming-towards-oneself is the meaning of existing in one's ownmost nullity.[42]

---

41 Esposito, 'L'impossibilità come trascendentale': 331.

42 Heidegger, *Being and Time*, pp. 378–79 [translation modified], cited in Esposito, 'L'impossibilità come trascendentale': 330. [Where the Macquarrie and Robinson translation renders *entschlossene* as 'resolute,' I have followed the Italian translation, which emphasizes de-cision as a kind of dis-closure. —Trans.]

5. Kant's *Opus Postumum*—a congeries of seemingly heterogenous jottings first partially published, and not without mistakes, only a century after the author's death—is perhaps the least studied of Kant's works. It is possible, however, as recent studies seem to suggest, in the wake of its definitive edition in volumes 21 and 22 of the *Akademie Ausgabe* (1936–38), to argue that it develops themes that on several points go further than the canonical system of the three *Critiques*.

We are interested here in the sections where Kant interrogates himself once again on the proper status of pure space and pure time, which in the classificatory table of the concept of nothing in the first *Critique* were registered under the formula *Ens imaginarium*, or 'Empty intuition without an object', and of the concept of noumenon, which the same table defined as *Ens rationis*, or 'Empty concept without an object'. While the other two forms of the concept of nothing—the *nihil privativum* (the simple negation of something, like shadow or cold) and the *nihil negativum* (mere contradiction, like the 'rectilinear figure with two sides')—are, as Kant puts it, only 'empty concepts' (*leere Begriffe*), the first two instead represent 'empty data for concepts' (*leere Data zu Begriffen*), almost as if in them, according to this paradoxical expression, something like a void were given to thought.

In the *Opus postumum*, Kant starts from this 'empty data' to thoroughly rethink the fundamental division of

the two sources of consciousness: receptivity and spontaneity, sensibility and intellect. If in the first an object is
given to us and in the second it is thought in relation to
representation, the crux of the *Critique* was that cognition
can only occur through the collaboration of these two originary sources. In the minute handwriting that fills the pages
of the *Opus*, Kant calls into question the two forms of the
nothing in which a void seems to give itself to sensibility
and thought. What is the status of an 'empty intuition without an object', as it is given in pure space and pure time,
and of an 'empty concept without an object', to wit the
noumenon? How can we think an objectless receptivity
that seems in some way to correspond to a spontaneity
that is equally devoid of an object?

Obsessively reprising, in countless variations, the definitions of space and time as forms of intuition, the annotations in fascicles VII and XI keep introducing new
elements that put these definitions into a new perspective.

> Space and time are not *objects* of intuition. For
> were they objects of intuition, they would be real
> things and require, in turn, another intuition in
> order to be represented to one as objects, and so
> on to infinity. Intuitions are not perceptions (that
> is, empirical) if they are pure, for that requires
> forces which determine the senses. How is it poss-
> ible, however, that pure intuitions yield, at the same

time, principles of perception—e.g. the attraction
of cosmic bodies? [Space and time are not *objects*
of intuition] but, rather, subjective forms of intuition itself, insofar as they contain a principle of
synthetic a priori propositions and of the possibility
of a transcendental philosophy; [they contain] phenomena prior to all perceptions.[43]

We should dwell here on a singular expression, which
would be meaningless according to the terms of the
Critique: 'phenomena prior to all perceptions
[*Erscheinungen vor allen Wahrnehmungen*]'. We are dealing
here with a phenomenality prior to all concrete experience,
almost as though something like a phenomenal dimension
could be given prior to possible experience, that is to say
prior to the phenomena that constitute the only possible
object of experience. Kant's notes do not tire of repeating
that space and time are not only forms of intuition, but
intuitions themselves, which, as such, provide a foundation
for axioms and synthetic a priori propositions, even if it is
not clear what is intuited in them, since, as pure intuitions,
they are by definition devoid of an object.

It is at this point that Kant introduces a concept as
decisive as it is problematic, which demands immediate
elucidation: 'phenomenon of the phenomenon' (*Erscheinung*

43 Immanuel Kant, *Opus Postumum* (Eckart Förster and Michael Rosen
trans, Eckart Förster ed.) (Cambridge: Cambridge University Press, 1993),
p. 159 [translation modified].

einer Erscheinung, also 'appearance of an appearance'). In space and time as pure intuitions and in the thing in itself, we are not directly dealing with phenomena, but with how the subject, in the experience of a phenomenon, is affected not by the object but by itself, by its own receptivity. If we do not simply represent to ourselves phenomena in space and time, but also space and time themselves as phenomena and sensible objects and if, in the physical sciences, we form concepts like aether and matter that are in no way given in empirical experience, that is because this, as it were, a priori phenomenality is grounded on an auto-affection of the subject.

The appearance of the appearance, Kant writes, is a representation of the formal through which 'the subject makes itself, according to a principle, into an object as it appears to itself—[that is,] as it affects itself and appears to itself, and extracts nothing more from intuition (the empirical) than it has inserted into it.'[44] 'The phenomenon of the phenomenon,' we read on another page, 'is the phenomenon

44 Kant, *Opus Postumum* (Förster and Rosen trans), pp. 116–17. [This is the closest passage I could locate in the English translation of the *Opus Postumum*. Agamben quotes from Vittorio Mathieu's Italian version (Bologna: Zanichelli, 1963), p. 176, which I translate here: 'the representation of the formal with which the subject affects itself according to a principle and is spontaneously an object for itself: this is no longer, in its turn, the empirical representation of the object and the phenomenon, but an a priori cognition of the sensible object, according to which the object does not draw from that ensemble anything more, by way of aggregate, than what it itself has put in it.' –Trans.]

of the subject affecting itself.' In fascicle VII, the same concept of auto-affection is employed regarding the thing in itself:

> The thing in itself is not another object, but another relation (*respectus*) of representation with the same subject, in order to think the latter not analytically, but synthetically, as the complex (*complexus*) of intuitive representations qua phenomena, in other words, representations that contain a solely subjective ground of determination of representations in the unity of intuition. The *ens rationis* = x is the positing of oneself according to the principle of identity, in which the subject is thought of as affecting itself [*als sich selbst afficirend*], and therefore in its form only as phenomenon.[45]

Another annotation defines this auto-affection of the subject as 'the phenomenon of the phenomenon': 'The indirect subjective phenomenon—in which the subject is for itself an object of empirical cognition and yet at the same time makes itself into an object of experience insofar as it affects itself—is the phenomenon of the phenomenon.'[46]

Let us reflect on this peculiar structure of a phenomenality that seems to precede the perception of phenomena.

---

45 I was unable to find this passage in the English translation, and have translated it directly from *Opus Postumum* (Mathieu trans.), p. 285. [Trans.]

46 English translation of the Italian version: *Opus Postumum* (Mathieu trans.), p. 285. [Trans.]

A note from fascicle VII details that space and time are given to us insofar as we are affected by objects qua phenomena:

> Space and time are not given objects of intuition, but themselves intuition—namely, pure, *a priori* intuition; yet they belong to us only insofar as we feel affected by objects, that is to say, when objects appear as simple phenomena. Not empirically, thus in a manner that contains the possibility of experience.[47]

In the givenness of space and time, which makes possible the experience of phenomena, we experience ourselves insofar as we are affected by objects, we are affected in some way by our own receptivity, and, in this way, we become an object for ourselves. As we read in another note from the same period: 'Space and time are therefore not objects of intuition [. . .] with them the subject constitutes itself into an object.'[48]

This clarifies the meaning of the paradoxical expression 'phenomenon of the phenomenon' (or 'appearance of the appearance') which Kant sometimes also defines as an 'indirect' or 'second-degree' phenomenon. The auto-affection that is at stake in it does not factually precede the

---

47 English translation of the Italian version: *Opus Postumum* (Mathieu trans.), p. 285. [Trans.]

48 English translation of the Italian version: *Opus Postumum* (Mathieu trans.), p. 277. [Trans.]

experience of phenomena but is implicit within them, while at the same time grounding their possibility in something like a phenomenality raised to the second power. What within auto-affection comes to appearance and is somehow given as phenomenon is the subject itself as the originary source of cognition, beyond its splitting into receptivity and spontaneity. As another annotation recites:

> The object of pure intuition, by means of which the subject posits itself, is infinite—namely, space and time. Intuition and concept belong to knowledge: that I am given to myself and thought by myself as object. Something exists (*apprehensio simplex*); I am not merely logical subject and predicate, but also object of *perception* (*dabile non solum cogitabile*).[49]

In this receptivity that affects itself, the two originary sources of cognition coincide without remainder: 'Positing and perception, spontaneity and receptivity, the objective and subjective relation, are simultaneous [*zugleich*]; because they are identical as to time, as appearances of how the subject is *affected*—thus are given in the same *actus* and are in progression towards experience (as a system of perceptions).'[50] The possibility of experience rests, in the final analysis, on an auto-affection.

---

49 Kant, *Opus Postumum* (Förster and Rosen trans), pp. 194–95.

50 Kant, *Opus Postumum* (Förster and Rosen trans), p. 132.

6. It is in this receptivity that suffers [*patisce*] itself that one could ground a theory of possibilities emancipated from every merely modal conception while also released from what we have called the ontological-political machine of the West. Possibility ceases to express the relation of an object to the faculty of cognition and, detaching itself at the same time from every relation of presupposition with regard to the act, presents itself instead as the experience of a subject affected by its own receptivity.

At the point where I experience my own receptivity, this experience is perfectly real; however, to the extent that it has no object other than itself, and that subject and object coincide within it, it also discloses the space of a pure possibility, in which life and the world for the first time become possible for me. A receptivity that suffers itself is, in this sense, the only adequate definition of a possibility that does not remain imprisoned in a merely logical-modal dimension, and of a power that has no need to realize itself and to transition to the act. Between power and act there is no passage: like the semiotic and the semantic according to Benveniste, they are co-originary and non-communicating.

Here the Aristotelian image of potential as a writing tablet on which nothing has yet been written assumes—if read correctly—its full pertinence. The observation by Alexander of Aphrodisias, according to whom what is at stake is not the tablet but the preparation of the sensitive wax that covers it, should be understood as an image of the auto-affection of receptivity: at the point where the writing tablet is and feels its own receptivity, its power is real without any need of a passage to the act; in the words of Albertus Magnus, 'it is as though the letters wrote themselves on the wax.'

When I experience a power in this sense, when I say, 'I can [*posso*] write', this in no way implies that I must realize a possibility that in itself is not real. 'I can write' does not mean that I have the power to write and consequently to realize in the act this power; it means that writing is for me immediately true and real, it is my form of life and not a power of which I would be the proprietor. If it were otherwise, if 'I can write' designated a power to write that must realize itself in the act, I would never be able to write, because from the act to power there is no passage. Possibility is generated contextually to the act and is inseparable from, but also irreducible to, it; in this sense, possibility is always *sub actu*. If when I feel, I feel myself feeling and am affected by my own receptivity, then this is for me altogether possible and at the same time real. And while effectivity is the state of powerless assignation to the factuality of beings, this experience coincides instead with the *conatus*, with the demand to persevere in one's being that, according to Spinoza, defines life.

If we now turn back to the theme from which we took our cue, we can say that the possible is the instance of an unrealizable in every real. Far from being what contains within itself an inclination towards realization, the possible is what resists realization and, in this way, it *can* what it is and *is* what it can. The splitting of the 'thing' of thought and language into power and act, essence and existence, which grounds the idea of a necessary passage from power to act, is instead in keeping with the ontological apparatus that conceives being and reality as a process of ceaseless realization. Not only does this conception entangle itself, as we have seen, in aporias and contradictions, but it ends up destroying—theoretically and practically, metaphysically and politically—the reality it wished to comprehend. Today, reality is in every domain undone by the processes of realization that should guarantee its consistency. Of course, a reality split into an unreal possibility and an effectivity that must be repeatedly realized lends itself to control and manipulation; however, precisely because—unmooring itself from its theological premises—realization is presupposed as continuous and interminable, the very possibility of a government of reality is revealed to be illusory.

And yet, on the basis of the concept of possibility that we have tried to define, there is another way of conceiving the 'thing' of thought, which rescues it from the fate that seemed to doom it to failure and catastrophe. The term 'thing' is often used, in philosophy as in ordinary speech, together with the anaphoric adjective 'itself' [*stesso*] (in the Latin sense of *ipse*): the thing itself, which in Plato's

Seventh Letter designates the most proper object of thought (*to pragma auto*). Prior to the thing as intentional correlate—abstract and always already divided—of language, prior to and alongside Heidegger's jug, inscribed into the poetic fourfold of earth and sky, gods and mortals, stands the thing itself, which corresponds to the experience of possibility that we have just defined. When, in the experience of a pure receptivity, a real possibility is disclosed, it coincides with the reality of the thing in its being manifest and sayable, prior to and beyond every splitting of power and act, essence and existence. The reality, the thinghood of the jug is not another thing: it is the jug itself in its opening, grasped in and by its inscription into the ontological apparatus, in and by its correlation with language. It is, in other words, an idea, the vision of a pure visibility, the knowledge of a pure knowability: a possibility that is as such perfectly unrealizable. The politics that cleaves to this unrealizable possibility is the only true politics.

The *Opus Postumum*'s notes on pure space and time, empty intuitions in which something like a matter is nevertheless given, can be read in connection with the Platonic doctrine of the *chora*, which the philosophical tradition has always seen as a theory of both place and matter. According to Kant, I can think a pure space and a matter only through an auto-affection, in which the subject is affected by its own receptivity. Even the 'difficult and obscure' definition of the *chora* that Plato offers in the *Timaeus* contains something like an auto-affection. Plato distinguishes three kinds of being: intelligible being, which is grasped with intelligence as a spontaneity that does not receive anything; sensible being, which is grasped with sensation (*met'aistheseos*); and *chora*, which is 'tangible through a kind of bastard reasoning accompanied by an absence of sensation (*meta anaistheseos*)'. What does 'perceiving with an absence of sensation' mean, if not experiencing, exactly as in Kant, the givenness of an empty intuition, of a pure receptivity with no object save for itself?

The Ancient Forest: Chora Space Matter

κἀγώ μοι δοκῶ μεμνημένος μάλα φοβεῖσθαι πῶς
χρὴ τηλικόνδε ὄντα διανεῦσαι τοιοῦτόν τε καὶ
τοσοῦτον πέλαγος λόγων

I too, when I think back, feel a good deal of
anxiety as to how at my age I am to make my way
across such a vast and formidable sea of words.

—PLATO, *Parmenides* 137a

Holy Plato, forgive us!
We have gravely sinned against you!

—FRIEDRICH HÖLDERLIN,
Preface to the penultimate edition of *Hyperion*

CHAPTER ONE

Silva

1. All we know about the author of a partial Latin translation of and commentary on Plato's *Timaeus* is his name: Calcidius. And yet it is thanks to this unknown—about whose dates we don't have any certainty (the mid-300s according to some, between the fourth and fifth centuries according to the editor of the monumental critical edition *in aedibus Instituti Warburgiani*)[1]—that the Middle Ages knew Plato. At least until Henry Aristippus' translation in the mid-twelfth century, Plato is essentially the *Timaeus* and the language of the dialogue's three interlocutors— Socrates, Critias and Timaeus, but a fourth is missing—is Calcidius' seemingly unassuming but in effect mannered and inventive Latin. Plato's fate—as some have perhaps too emphatically suggested—was for a long time in the

---

1 Calcidius, *Timaeus a Calcidio translatus commentarioque instructus* (J. H. Waszink ed.), Plato Latinus, VOL. 4 (London: Warburg Institute, 1962).

hands of this unknown. While his translation and commentary only concerned the first part of the *Timaeus*, Calcidius' book had such wide circulation from the eleventh century onwards that it has been noted there was no medieval library without its copy (the translation of approximately a fourth of Plato's dialogue begun by Cicero is attested in a mere three codices, by contrast with Calcidius' one hundred and ninety-eight). Even in the age of humanism, Petrarch and Pico della Mirandola each owned a copy, both feverishly annotated in the margins, and it is probable that Dante read it with equal care during his own wanderings. Calcidius is especially cognizant of the dignity and difficulty of his task as translator which he defines, in the dedication to 'his [Bishop] Osius [of Corduba]', as a 'hitherto unattempted work' and a *res ardua*, a difficult matter.[2] That is why, conscious that 'the simulacrum of a recondite writing'—namely, a translation— risks being even more obscure than the original, he has decided to append to it a commentary, in which he moreover inserts a brief treatise on obscurity. If 'many discourses are true but obscure', that *obscuritas* may stem from the intention of the author, the incapacity of his audience or the nature of the matter at hand; but since in the case in question 'the Timaeus who conducts the discussion is not

---

2 Calcidius, *On Plato's 'Timaeus'* (John Magee ed. and trans.) (Cambridge, MA: Harvard University Press, 2016), p. 3.

a faltering speaker, and his audience is not sluggish,'[3] it follows that the obscurity derives from the argument's inherent difficulty. Like Cavalcanti's esoteric song, which can be read only by 'people who have the understanding' (*da le persone ch'anno intendimento*),[4] even the *Timaeus* 'has been, and is perceived to have been, devised almost exclusively for those who are versed in the use and application of all such sciences'[5] (namely, as Calcidius had detailed: arithmetic, astronomy, geometry and music).

What Calcidius' commentary is concerned with in the final part of his book is Plato's theory of matter, which is undoubtedly so demanding that it cannot be '*plainly* or transparently intimated.'[6] It is in order to render into Latin this unapproachable concept that Calcidius displays his unmatched genius as a translator: in his commentary, he translates the Greek *hyle* (and the other terms which, according to him, Plato employs to express matter) with the term *silva*, 'jungle, forest'.

---

3 Calcidius, *On Plato's 'Timaeus'*, p. 627.

4 Cavalcanti's song is entitled 'Donna mi prega perch'io voglio dire' (A lady asks me—I speak for such reason). [Trans.]

5 Calcidius, *On Plato's 'Timaeus'*, p. 127.

6 Calcidius, *On Plato's 'Timaeus'*, p. 627.

2. The choice by this otherwise unknown translator is particularly remarkable in that it cannot really be defined as an act of fidelity or betrayal. The fact is that the term *hyle* does not appear in the *Timaeus*, except for once, in a passage (69a) that does not belong to the section translated by Calcidius, where it is used metaphorically to signify the part of the argument that remains to be treated ('now that there lie before us, like the wood for some craftsmen [*oia tektosin emin hyle*], the two kinds of cause'). To designate what his pupil Aristotle will call *hyle*, in the technical-philosophical sense of matter, in the dialogue Plato employs a term, *chora*, which signifies 'space, territory, region', and which Calcidius in fact consistently renders with *locus*. It was Aristotle who identified *chora* with matter. In the *Physics*, he commandingly affirms, albeit with no textual basis, that 'Plato [. . .] says in the *Timaeus* argues that matter [*hyle*] and space [*chora*] are one and the same thing'.[7] Our unknown translator knows this so well that when, at the beginning of the last part of his commentary, which some codices record under the heading *De silva*, the time comes to justify his translation, he can shrewdly write:

> Since these bodies cannot exist on their own, per se, or without a substance to engender them from within itself (which [Plato] variously calls the

7 Aristotle, *Physics: Books III and IV* (Edward Hussey ed. and trans.) (Oxford: Clarendon Press, 1983), p. 23 (209b11–16).

mother [*matrem*], *nurse* [*nutricula*], *womb* [*gre-mium*] *of all generation*, and *Place* [*locum*], and later thinkers [*iunores*, namely, the Platonist phil-osophers who came before Calcidius, about whom he often displays his mistrust—G. A.] call *hyle*, and we *silva* [*nos silvam vocamus*].[8]

To this inventory of the Platonic terms for matter also belongs 'necessity', about which Calcidius writes, a few pages before: '*Necessity* (*necessitas*) [. . .] is what [Plato] uses here to designate *hyle*, which we can call *silva* in Latin (*quam nos Latine silvam possumus nominare*).'[9] Earlier still, commenting on a passage in the dialogue where it is said that the earth is the oldest of the divinities, Calcidius had written 'after chaos, which the Greeks call *hyle* and we call *silva*.'[10] *Silva*, to render Plato's supposed matter, is therefore an invention as felicitous as it is arbitrary: in keeping with one of the metaphorical meanings of the term in Latin, it gathers up in a single word a veritable forest of terms.

3. To gauge the originality of the choice made by our unknown commentator, we should recall that Latin pres-ented a term—*materia* or *materies*—that had been used to

---

8 Calcidius, *On Plato's 'Timaeus'*, p. 553.

9 Calcidius, *On Plato's 'Timaeus'*, p. 545.

10 Calcidius, *On Plato's 'Timaeus'*, p. 325.

render both the Greek *hyle* in a philosophical register as well as the *chora* of the *Timaeus*. As Cicero writes: 'Plato holds the view that the world was made by god out of an all-containing matter [*ex materia omnia in se recipiente*].'[11] Apuleius confirms this no less firmly with reference to the *Timaeus*: 'Plato therefore thought there were three principles of things, God, matter and the forms of things [*deum et materiam rerumque formas*].'[12] Even if he occasionally employs this term (*silva atque materies*),[13] Calcidius prefers a term which, while it renders the vegetal meaning of the Greek perfectly, could seem ill-suited to express matter's new philosophical vocation. That said, the term *silva* was used in rhetoric to designate something that could be related to the matter or argument of an oration. Quintilian tells us of the vice of those who, forgetting that the pen should be 'slow, but precise', get through the matter at hand as fast as possible, writing extemporaneously (*ex tempore*) according to 'heat and impulse': 'they call this draft', he adds, 'their "raw material" [*hanc silvam vocant*].'[14] Cicero

---

11 Cicero, *Academica*, BOOK 2, §118 in *On the Nature of the Gods. Academics* (H. Rackham trans.) (Cambridge, MA: Harvard University Press, 1933), p. 619 [translation modified].

12 Apuleius, *On the Doctrines of the Philosophy of Plato*, 1.5.190, in *The Metamorphosis, or Golden Ass, and Philosophical Works* (Thomas Taylor trans.) (London: Robert Triphook and Thomas Rodd, 1822), p. 324.

13 Calcidius, *On Plato's 'Timaeus'*, p. 642.

14 Quintilian, *Institutio Oratoria*, BOOK 10, CHAP. 3, §17, in *The Orator's Education, Volume IV: Books 9–10* (Donald A. Russell ed. and trans.) (Cambridge, MA: Harvard University Press, 2002).

himself employs the term to signify the overabundance of a discourse: *rerum est silva magna* [there is a large stock of ideas];[15] *omnis enim ubertas et quasi silva dicendi* [for all richness of style, and what may be called the raw material of oratory].[16] There is a forest in words, just as there is a forest of trees and scrub. The unknown commentator could hardly ignore these meanings of the term, just as he undoubtedly knew that Statius had entitled one of his collections of poetry *Silvae*, probably alluding to the variety and multiplicity of the themes it touched on (this is also the sense in which the term appears as the title of a section in Eugenio Montale's third and most important collection, *The Storm*). In every instance, a Latin ear could perceive in the word *silva* an overabundance, obscurity and density that were well suited to the new concept of matter that the end of the ancient world, via an apocryphal attribution to Plato, bequeathed to the Middle Ages.

---

15 Cicero, *On the Orator*, BOOK 3, §93, in *On the Orator: Book 3. On Fate. Stoic Paradoxes. Divisions of Oratory* (H. Rackham trans.) (Cambridge, MA: Harvard University Press, 1942), pp. 74–75.

16 Cicero, *Orator*, §12, in *Brutus. Orator* (G. L. Hendrickson and H. M. Hubbell trans) (Cambridge, MA: Harvard University Press, 1971), pp. 314–15.

4. Eight centuries later, Calcidius' sylvan choice would enjoy an unexpected sequel in the Platonist school of Chartres. One of the most singular personalities in the school—about whose life we know as little as with Calcidius—was so seduced by the *silva* of the Latinized *Timaeus* as to draw from it his own name: Bernardus 'Silvester', that is to say, 'material'. Both philosopher and poet, the author of a tragedy (*Mathematicus*) which is a cathartic remake of sorts of *Oedipus Rex*, Bernardus composed a prosimetrum entitled *Cosmographia* or *De universitate mundi* where what is at stake, as in the *Timaeus*, is the origin and structure of the universe. Both as a poet and as a philosopher, Bernardus professes a poetics of the figure or the envelope (*involucrum*), which divides into two species: allegory, which concerns the 'divine page' and the *integumentum*, the 'covering' or 'disguise', the proper form of philosophy, which 'hides the true in obscure figures'.[17] That is why he disguises philosophical concepts as characters, the first of which is indeed Silva, who unlike the others—Nature, Nous, Physis, Providence—remains mute throughout the book, while the others don't stop talking about her. What Silvester wants to highlight about *Silva* is above all its ambiguity and overabundance: 'intractable, a formless chaos, a hostile coalescence [*concretio*

---

17 Bernardus Silvestris, *Cosmografia e Commento a Marziano Capella* in Thierry of Chartres, William of Conches and Bernardus Silvestris, *Il divino e il megacosmo: Testi filosofici e scientifici della scuola di Chartres* (Enzo Maccagnolo ed.) (Milan: Rusconi, 1980), pp. 554–55.

pugnax], pallid face of substance [*discolor usiae vultus*], mass discordant with itself [*sibi dissona massa*] [...] turbulence,'[18] and, at the same time, 'the inexhaustible womb of generation, the primary basis of formal existence, the matter of all bodies, the foundation of substance.'[19] Nous, to bring order to the formless, must vanquish its malice (*malum Silvae*) and yet '[n]o small honour and thanks are due to Silva, who contains the original natures of things diffused through her vast womb. Within this cradle the infant universe squalls, and cries to be clothed with a finer appearance.'[20] In the end, once chaos has been tamed, the forest can be called 'with its true name: world', and be ordered into the splendid figure of things.

An echo of this ambiguity may be plausibly discerned in the most illustrious descendant of Calcidius' *silva*: Dante's forest. The 'ancient forest' of the earthly paradise literally evokes the *antiquior silva* of the unknown commentator (*unam quandam antiquiorem communem omnium silvam* [a particular, unique *silva* prior and common to all]);[21] but since the 'dark forest' in which the poet finds himself at the start of the *Divine Comedy* is, as Dante does not tire of intimating, the Edenic forest itself, in which the 'root of

---

18 Bernardus Silvestris, *Cosmographia* (Winthrop Wetherbee ed. and trans.) (New York: Columbia University Press, 1990), p. 67.

19 Bernardus Silvestris, *Cosmographia*, p. 70.

20 Bernardus Silvestris, *Cosmographia*, p. 68.

21 Calcidius, *On Plato's 'Timaeus'*, pp. 580–81.

mankind's tree was guiltless' (*in cui fu innocente l'umana radice*),[22] it is legitimate to suppose that the forest in which Dante goes astray is, among other things, the *silva* of matter. However, once his reason has been purified ('Now is your will upright, wholesome and free'; *libero, dritto e sano è il tuo arbitrio*),[23] the forest is restored to its primordial innocence, so much so that it can be figured by a dancing girl in love, the first letters of whose name (Matelda) coincide with those of matter [*materia*]. Matter is both the dark forest of sin and 'the heavenly forest thick with living green' (*divina foresta spessa e viva*),[24] in which humanity can recover its natural justice.

It is worth correcting the widespread opinion according to which Calcidius is a Christian author.[25] As has been noted, Calcidius never cites the New Testament or Christian authors while he demonstrates good knowledge of Jewish culture and the Old Testament, which he quotes not only according to the Septuagint but—which is hardly commonplace—from the versions by Aquila of Sinope and Symmachus.[26] In the only passage where, with reference to the negative influence of the star Sirius, he evokes—

---

22 Dante, *Purgatory*, CANTO 28, LINE 142, p. 304.

23 Dante, *Purgatory*, canto 27, line 140, p. 294.

24 Dante, *Purgatory*, canto 28, line 2, p. 300.

25 Calcidius, *Timaeus a Calcidio translatus commentarioque instructus* (Waszink ed.), pp. *xi–xii*; Calcidius, *Commentario al 'Timeo' di Platone* (Claudio Moreschini ed.) (Milan: Bompiani, 2003), p. *xxxi*.

26 Calcidius, *On Plato's 'Timaeus'*, p. 557.

generically and without citing his source—an episode (*historia*)
from the Gospels (the star that heralds 'the descent of a venerable
God to bestow the grace of salvation upon mankind and mortal
beings'),[27] he unequivocally attributes familiarity with this 'story'
to Osius and not to himself ('You know perfectly well').[28] If he
had wanted to attest to his Christian faith, he could have used a
formula such as 'we know them,' while the unexpected invocation
of the Christian dedicatee of the book is a discreet but unmis-
takable way of declaring his own foreignness to Christianity. It
is possible that, as his name indicates, he hailed from a Jewish
community in Chalcis, were the presence of a Greek-speaking
community of Jews is attested by multiple testimonies.

5. Having reached the decisive juncture in the dialogue, in
which Plato defines the status of *chora* as a 'third kind' of
being next to the intelligible and the sensible, Calcidius
becomes aware that he is faced with 'a certain remarkable
conception in mind [*mira quadam animi conceptione*]',[29]
in which 'the loftiness of the mind [or rather of the chest,
altitudinem pectoris—G. A.]'[30] of the authors has distilled
into few words (*brevi elocutione*) what he thought—or

27 Calcidius, *On Plato's 'Timaeus'*, p. 331.

28 Calcidius, *On Plato's 'Timaeus'*, p. 341.

29 Calcidius, *On Plato's 'Timaeus'*, p. 667.

30 Calcidius, *On Plato's 'Timaeus'*, p. 667 [translation modified].

suspected, since in what concerns the forest only conjec-
tures are possible (here Calcidius twice employs the term
suspicio). The commentator dwells for almost two pages
on the problematic expression with which Timaeus tries
to encompass the specificity of *chora*: 'tangible with an
absence of sensation [*met'anaisthesias apton*]', which, taking
some license, he had in turn translated as *ipsum sine sensu
tangentis tangitur* ('is itself tangible independently of any
sensory experience on the part of the one who comes into
contact with it').[31] Perception, he observes, is the perception
of certain and definite things, which possess form and
quality, while the forest is something indefinite, devoid of
form and figure; therefore, we cannot imagine it with sensation but only *sine sensu*. And yet—and here the language
of the unknown commentator displays its subtlety—'a certain faint form of contact with it occurs in the absence of
touching [*fit tamen evanida quaedam eius attrectatio sine
contagio*],'[32] in which we do not touch the forest, but the
bodies within it, such that 'when the latter are perceived a
suspicion of its being perceived arises [*quae cum sentiuntur,
suspicio nascitur ipsam sentiri*]'.[33] The perception of matter
cannot but be obscure and it is not a sense, but a con-
sensus, a co-sensation that accompanies the clear sensation
of bodies. Therefore,

---

31 Calcidius, *On Plato's 'Timaeus'*, p. 117.

32 Calcidius, *On Plato's 'Timaeus'*, p. 669.

33 Calcidius, *On Plato's 'Timaeus'*, p. 669.

since [. . .] material things [*silvestria*] are perceived
whereas matter [*silva*] is not perceived in its proper
nature but because of the material things [*silvestria*] is thought to be perceived along with them,
there occurs an uncertain perception of the sort
described, and it is said that matter [*silvam*] is tangible independently of any sensory experience on
the part of those who come into contact with it.[34]

What happens here is

as if one were to say that darkness too is visible
independently of any sensory experience [*ut si
quis dicat tenebras quoque sine sensu videri*]. For
the vision of a person who gazes upon darkness is
not comparable to his normal experience of gazing
upon distinctly colored objects, but owing to a
contrary affection, an absence or want of the things
which the eyes see (for darkness is colorless and
lacks the illumination of light), his vision is in a
position, not to comprehend any quality in the
darkness, but to suspect the fact of nonbeing but
not the existence of any particular reality, and
despite seeing nothing he thinks he is actually
seeing what he does not see [*videtur videre quod
non videt*] and supposes he is seeing something
although he sees nothing (for what vision is there

---

34 Calcidius, *On Plato's 'Timaeus'*, p. 669.

in darkness?) [. . .] In some such way, then,
although matter [*silva*] too is tangible [*contigua*],
in that it is believed to be touched [*contingi*] even
though the objects of touch in the primary sense
come under the senses, in fact our contact with it
occurs incidentally; but the experience itself is
independent of any sensory experience because
matter in itself and on its own is imperceptible by
either touch or the other senses.[35]

The comparison between the 'suspicion' of matter and
vision in the dark derives from Plotinus who, commenting
on the passage in question in the *Timaeus*, had likened
darkness to the perception of matter, writing:

What, then, is the soul's [state of] indefiniteness?
Is it complete unknowing and aphasia? Or does
indeterminacy rather consist in a certain positive
discourse [*en katafasei tini*]? Just as darkness serves
the eye as matter for every unseen colour, so too
the soul, when it has removed everything luminous
in perceptible things and is no longer able to define
the residue, is in a state like seeing in the dark,
and becomes somehow assimilated to what it vir-
tually sees.[36]

---

35 Calcidius, *On Plato's 'Timaeus'*, pp. 669–71.

36 Plotinus, *Ennead II.4: On Matter* (A. A. Long ed. and trans.) (Las Vegas
NV: Parmenides, 2022), p. 63.

Following and simplifying after his own fashion Plotinus'
text (which appropriately had been entitled *On the Two
Matters* by his editor Porphyry), our unknown commentator had oriented his exegesis of the Platonic script through
an image that the mystical tradition had already used and
would constantly take up again every time it was a question
of describing the knowledge—or, rather, unknowing [*inco-
noscenza*] (Plotinus employs the terms *anoia* and *aphasia*)—of the ineffable. It is possible, however, that Timaeus'
words are after all not so enigmatic and that Calcidius'
tenebrous metaphor contributed to lastingly leading astray
the interpretation of an undoubtedly decisive passage in
the dialogue, which we must therefore endeavour to inter-
pret from scratch.

CHAPTER TWO

Chora

1. That the problem of *chora* in the *Timaeus* is, to say the least, obscure is a commonplace that both ancient and modern interpreters never tire of reminding us about. This judgement, after all, appears to be authorized by Plato himself, who defines *chora* as 'a kind that is difficult and vague' (*kalepon kai amydron eidos*)[1] and places on Timaeus' lips a curious theory which—since 'the accounts we give of things have the same character [*syggeneis*, from the same family— G. A.] as the subjects they set forth discourses are akin'[2]— appears to justify the obscurity and incoherence of the exposition in terms of the particular nature of the theme at hand. That said, we should not forget that obscurity is an integral part of the 'art of writing' and that an apparently enigmatic discourse may conceal a perfectly clear meaning.

---

1 Plato, *Timaeus* (Donald J. Zeyl trans.) (Indianapolis, IN: Hackett, 2020), p. 38 (49a).

2 Plato, *Timaeus* (Zeyl trans.), p. 15 (29b).

A more attentive reading of the passage in question shows
that Platonic esotericism does not issue here into a justifi-
cation of vagueness but that, on the contrary, the expository
form chosen by Timaeus is the one that allows the greatest
possible clarity. Timaeus in fact distinguishes between two
kinds of discourse: the first, which concerns the paradigm,
must like the latter be immobile (*monimos, akinetos*) and
firm (*bebaios*), while the second, which regards the image,
must instead have the latter's verisimilitude (*eikotas*, the
correspondence is forcefully signalled by the alliteration
*eikonos eikotas: ontos de eikonos eikotas ana logon te ekeinon
ontas*, 'since discourses of what is an image, will by analogy
be imaginal').[3] If the second discourse will definitely not be
'irrefutable' like the first, it will nevertheless convey its
meaning in the most persuasive manner, as Timaeus makes
sure to underscore: 'Instead, if we can come up with
accounts no less [*medenos etton*] likely than any, we ought
to be content.'[4] The formula *medenos etton*, nonetheless,
which firmly signals an opposition, is all the more significant
inasmuch as it will be explicitly reprised when the time
comes to move to the exposition of *chora*: 'I shall keep to
what I stated at the beginning, the virtue of likely accounts,
and so shall try right from the start to say about things,
both individually and collectively, what is no less likely than

3 Or, as Zeyl translates, 'accounts of what is a likeness, are themselves
likely'. Plato, *Timaeus* (Zeyl trans.), p. 15 (29c). [Trans.]

4 Plato, *Timaeus* (Zeyl trans.), p. 15 (29d).

any, more likely, in fact [*medenos etton eikota, mallon de*], than what I have said before'.[5] Far from implying—as an exegetical tradition going back to Calcidius insists on incautiously repeating—a guessing in the dark about what something is not rather than what something is, Timaeus' methodological premise demands, in a manner compatible with its object, the greatest possible perspicuity. The formula 'a kind that is difficult and vague [*kelpon kai amydron eidos*]', so often cited to certify an inevitable obscurity (though *amydron* does not really mean 'obscure' but difficult to make out or to read: *amydra*, illegible, are above all the *grammata*, letters), takes on its true meaning only when it is restored to the perspective of this demand: 'our account [*logos*] compels us to attempt to illuminate [*enphanisai*] in words [*logois*] a kind that is difficult and vague'.[6]

The attributes through which Timaeus defines the intelligible paradigm are also not necessarily positive ones. *Akinetos*, immobile, is used by the Stranger in *The Sophist* to mock the immobility of Parmenidean being: 'having mind, life and soul, will it stay, animated as it is, absolutely immobile [*akinetos . . . estanai*]?' (249a). That the distinction between the two kinds of discourses does not imply a hierarchical relation is also proven by the passage that immediately follows this one. Having affirmed that the discourses on the image will be akin to the image by analogy,

---

5 Plato, *Timaeus* (Zeyl trans.), p. 37 (48d).
6 Plato, *Timaeus* (Zeyl trans.), p. 15 (29c).

Timaeus adds that 'in proportion to the previous accounts, that is, what *ousia* is to generation, truth is to faith [*otiper pros genesin ousia, touto pros pistin aletheia*]'.[7] The meaning of this assertion is clarified if we relate it to the passage from the *Republic* which it partially cites. There, Plato is constructing a theory of the forms of knowledge that culminate in the dialectic: reserving the name of science for the dialectic, he employs the name *dianoia* to distinguish geometry and similar disciplines from the latter, while distinguishing them in turn from faith or belief (*pistis*) and imagination (*eikasia*). 'The last two taken together', he adds at this point,

> we call opinion [*doxa*], the other two, intellect [*noesis*].
> [. . .] And as being [*ousia*] is to becoming, so intellect
> [*noesis*] is to opinion [*doxan*], and as intellect is to
> opinion, so knowledge [*epistemen*] is to faith and dia-
> noetic thinking to imagination.[8]

It has rightly been observed that *pistis* thus comes to occupy, in the sphere of opinion, the same rank belonging to *episteme* in the domain of *noesis*.[9] If intellection via the dialectic is alone in being capable of grasping essence, Socrates' exposition does not aim so much at establishing a hierarchy but rather at avoiding both the confusion of the modalities of knowledge and, as we read in the *Republic* (534c), the attempt to grasp through opinion that idea of the Good that can only be the object of science. In

7 Plato, *Timaeus* (Zeyl trans.), p. 15 [translation modified].

8 Plato, *Republic* (Grube and Reeve trans), p. 1149 (533e) [translation modified].

9 Angelica Taglia, *Il concetto di pistis in Platone* (Rome: Le Lettere, 1998); J. L. Stocks, 'The Divided Line of *Plato Rep. VI*', *The Classical Quarterly*, 5(2) (1911): 73–88.

the *Timaeus*, the parallelism between the two forms of knowledge—of the intelligible and of the sensible—is even more
marked: they are clearly distinguished but not hierarchically
ordered. This is the sense in which we should read the thesis
according to which what *ousia* is with respect to genesis, truth is
with respect to *pistis*. And that, in the latter's proper sphere,
beliefs (*pisteis*) are in their own way 'firm and true' (*bebaioi kai
aletheis*) is stated unreservedly about the soul of the world: 'whenever the account concerns anything that is perceptible [. . .]
firm and true opinions and convictions come about. Whenever,
on the other hand, the account concerns any object of reasoning
[. . .] the necessary result is understanding and knowledge
[*nous episteme te*]'.[10] We can say, from this perspective, that
modernity begins when, starting with Descartes, certainty and
science are dislocated into the extraneous sphere of the knowledge of the sensible world.

The reading of the Platonic doctrine of *chora* has been influenced
in recent decades by the homonymous essay by Jacques Derrida
published in 1987. This text is particularly interesting because
the author, in a characteristic gesture, employs the term to provide
not so much, and not only, an acute exegesis of the *Timaeus*, but
a kind of lucid auto-interpretation of his own thought. Among
the essay's merits is no doubt that of having forcefully underscored the exceptionality and irreducibility of the concept, but
the emphasis is pushed to the point of negating its very conceptual character. The names that *chora* receives in the *Timaeus*

---

10 Plato, *Timaeus* (Zeyl trans.), p. 23 (37b–c).

do not designate an essence, the stable being of an eidos, since *chora* is neither of the order of the eidos nor of the order of mimemes, that is, of images of the eidos which come to imprint themselves in it—which thus *is not* and does not belong to the two known or recognized genera of being. It is not, and this nonbeing cannot but be *declared*, that is, be caught or conceived. [...] She 'is' nothing other than the sum or the process of what has just been inscribed 'on' her, on the subject of her, on her subject, right up against her subject, but she is not the *subject* or the *present support* of all these interpretations, even though, nevertheless, she is not reducible to them. [...] This absence of support, which cannot be translated into absent support or into absence as support, provokes *and* resists any binary or dialectical determination, any inspection of a philosophical *type*, or let us say, more rigorously, of an *ontological* type.[11]

The analogy with the definition (or rather the description) that Derrida gives of the fundamental terms of his thought like *différance* or 'trace' is patent: 'What *differance*, the *trace*, and so on "mean"—which hence does not mean anything—is "before" the concept, the name, the word, "something" that would be nothing, that no longer arises from Being, from presence or from the presence of the present, nor even from absence.'[12] *Chora* thus becomes

---

11 Jacques Derrida, 'Khōra' (Ian McLeod trans.) in *On the Name* (Thomas Dutoit ed.) (Stanford, CA: Stanford University Press, 1995), pp. 95, 99–100. [I have modified quotations from Derrida, employing Agamben's transliteration of the Greek as *chora* not *khōra*. —Trans.]

12 Jacques Derrida, 'How to Avoid Speaking: Denials' (Ken Frieden trans.) in *Derrida and Negative Theology* (Harold Coward and Toby Foshay eds) (Albany, NY: State University of New York Press, 1992), p. 79.

the negative foundation that makes it possible to articulate with unusual clarity the very principles of the deconstructive method:

> We would never claim to propose the exact word, the *mot juste*, for *chora*, nor to name it, *itself*, over and above all the turns and detours of rhetoric, nor finally to approach it, *itself*, for what it will have been, outside of any point of view, outside of any anachronic perspective. Its name is not an exact word, not a *mot juste*. It is promised to the ineffaceable even if what it names, *chora*, is not reduced to its name. Tropology and anachronism are inevitable. And all we would like to show is that it is structure which makes them thus inevitable, makes of them some-thing other than accidents, weaknesses, or provisional moments. It is this structural law which seems to me never to have been approached *as such* by the whole history of interpretations of the *Timaeus*.[13]

That this 'structural law' coincides with the author's method is what he appears to be discreetly suggesting. Having become a name 'deprived of a real referent [*privé de référent réel*]',[14] the term *chora* can thus be isolated from its function in the dialogue—that of explaining the genesis of the sensible cosmos—to be transformed into the condition of possibility of every deconstructive practice. We could say that deconstruction can take place, with its tropology and anachronisms, because there is *chora*. The non-concept of *chora* is situated here, with regard to the tradition of Greek philosophy, just like *différance*, the trace and *espacement* in deconstruction. Derrida can thus write that

---

13 Derrida, 'Khōra', pp. 93–94.

14 Derrida, 'Khōra', p. 97.

his 'interpretation of the uninterpretable *chora*' coincides with what he has attempted faithfully to think concerning the Greek inheritance.[15] So it is not by chance that the name *chora* appears for the first time in the 1968 essay 'Plato's Pharmacy', in which Derrida develops his theory of the originary supplement on the basis of a reading of Plato. As has been noted, the reading of the *Timaeus* advanced in Derrida's essay converges in this sense with negative theology and has hardly served to refute the obscurity traditionally ascribed to the dialogue.

2. If the *Timaeus* can therefore no longer be considered, according to St Jerome's malicious formula, the *obscurissimus Platonis liber*, 'which not even Cicero's golden lips could manage to make legible',[16] its interpretation will nonetheless need to stick all the more closely to the subtleties of the exposition and the text's terminological choices, in order to comprehend all of its strategic implications. The first problem to tackle is the resoluteness of Plato's choice to call with the far from obvious term *chora* the 'difficult and uncertain idea' that he intends to define. The question is especially delicate because beginning with Aristotle a long exegetical tradition has constantly identified matter with *chora* (and the latter with the place, *topos*; *Physics*

---

15 Jacques Derrida, 'We Other Greeks' (Pascale-Anne Brault and Michael Naas trans) in *Derrida and Antiquity* (Miriam Leonard ed.) (Oxford: Oxford University Press, 2010), p. 36.

16 St Jerome, *Commentary on Amos* 2.5.283 [Trans.]

209b11–16). If for Plotinus this identity was so trivial that he could include without the least hesitation his analysis of *chora* in his treatise *On the Two Matters*, in the twentieth century one of the highest authorities on Greek thought, Carlo Diano, could still entitle his particularly acute reading 'The Problem of Matter in Plato: *Chora* in the *Timaeus*'.[17] When ancient commentators interrogate Plato's terminological choice, they briskly respond that he used the term metaphorically (*metaphorikos*) or by analogy (*kata analogian*), because the place—which Plato moreover has left undefined—receives bodies just as matter does.[18]

The thing is that the other names with which Timaeus tries to specify the nature of the *chora* appear to confirm the analogy. This 'third kind' or principle—next to the intelligible 'which is forever and immutable' and the sensible 'which becomes and is visible'—is above all defined as 'receptacle' or 'asylum' (*hypodoche*, like the verb *dechomai* whence it derives, belongs to the lexicon of welcome and hospitality, and Thucydides uses it for the asylum offered to fugitive slaves; 49a6), as well as 'what receives all bodies' (*ta panta dechomenos somata*; 50b5) or 'all genera' (*to ta*

---

17 Carlo Diano, 'Il problema della materia in Platone: la chora del Timeo', *Giornale critico della filosofia italiana* 49 (1979): 321–35.

18 See Simplicius, *On Aristotle Physics 4.1–5 and 10–14* (J. O. Urmson trans.), Ancient Commentators on Aristotle (Richard Sorabji series ed.) (London: Bloomsbury, 2014), p. 34 (540.22–29), who does not himself speak of metaphors but underscores the real proximity between place and matter.

panta ekdexomenon en autoi gene; 50e5). That is why it is likened to a mother (*proseikasai to men dechomenon metri*; 50d2), but before that to a wet nurse (*tithene*; at 49a6 the term is coupled with *hypodoche*: the third kind gives hospitality and nourishment). Even more compelling is the analogy with matter in the passage where *chora* is ultimately compared to a mould or print-bearer (*ekmageion*):

> Suppose you were moulding gold [*ek chrysou*] into every shape there is, going on nonstop remoulding one shape into the next. If someone then were to point at one of them and ask you, 'What is it?', your safest answer by far, with respect to truth, would be to say, 'gold' [. . .] Now the same account holds also for that nature which receives all the bodies. We must always refer to it by the same term, for it does not depart from its own power [*dynamis*] in any way. Not only does it always receive all things, it has never in any way whatever taken on any form similar to any of the things that enter it. Its nature is to be [*keitai*, to lie] [like] a mould for everything, and it is modified, shaped, and reshaped by the things that enter it. These are the things that make it appear different at different times.[19]

It is possible that this was the passage on which Aristotle based his otherwise legitimate assertion according to which Plato had identified *chora* with matter, as well as his definition of *hyle* as 'what lies beneath' (*hypokeimenon*). In any case, it is noteworthy that modern interpreters continue to see in the spatiality of *chora* something akin to matter. As a shrewd scholar of Platonism writes: 'The spatial medium (*chora*) is both "that in which phenomena appear" and "what they are constituted by" so that the ambiguity of the term *chora* is the result of the relative lack of distinction between its constitutive and its spatial aspects'[20] (this is tantamount to repeating, almost verbatim, Proclus' judgement in his commentary to the *Timaeus*, according to which matter is both place and constitutive element, 'the "out of which" and "in which" [*ex ou e en oi*]').[21]

It is striking that critics have not asked themselves how such an obvious analogy could have been missed by Plato. It is often repeated that Plato did not know the term *hyle* in the sense of matter. And yet not only can the sole instance of *hyle* in the *Timaeus* be accorded the generic sense of 'material' (*tekton* does not just designate the carpenter or shipwright, but more generically any artisan who does not work with metals), but a simple consultation of Friedrich

---

20 Luc Brisson, *Le même et l'autre dans la structure ontologique du 'Timée' de Platon* (Paris: Klincksieck, 1974).

21 Proclus, *Commentary on Plato's 'Timaeus', Volume II, Book 2: Proclus on the Causes of the Cosmos and its Creation* (David T. Runia and Michael Share eds and trans) (Cambridge: Cambridge University Press, 2008), p. 217 (357.13–14).

Ast's *Lexicon platonicum* and of Édouard Des Places' more recent volume shows that the meaning of matter is always listed alongside that of forest and timber (six times in Ast and three in Des Places). If the occurrence in the *Philebus* ('medicines and all the instruments and every kind of matter [*pasan hylen*] are available to all with the aim of producing'; 54c2), seems to dispel any doubts, in the *Laws* (705c1), Plato appears intentionally to associate the term *hyle* (in the sense of 'timber or construction material') with *chora* and *topos*, almost as if to signal both their closeness and their difference: 'which material [or timber] for the construction of ships [*naupegesimes hyles*] furnishes the place of our territory [*o topos emin tes choras*]?'

Because Plato, albeit plausibly aware of the analogy between the two terms (or three, if we include *topos*), resolutely opted for only one of them, the most elementary philological care should lead us to interrogate the reasons for this choice rather than limiting ourselves to acknowledging the substantial semantic overlap. If Plato, invalidating Proclus' judgement, privileged 'being-in' (49e7: 'that in which [*en hoi*] all things that are generated manifest themselves and destroy themselves anew'; 50d7: 'that in which [*en hoi*] something is generated') against the 'being-from' (*ek hou*), and furthermore distinguished the being-in of the *chora* from that of the place, only a careful consideration of the Platonic usage of these terms can make sense of their supposed identification in the tradition that Aristotle has bequeathed to modernity.

The habit of projecting the Aristotelian interpretation onto the very text of the dialogue is so unyielding that a good number of readings of the *Timaeus*, ancient as well as modern, turn out to be meticulous exegeses of *Physics* 209, 11–16 and 33–35, which analyse the two theses contained in those passages as though they were Plato's own words. Aristotle affirms, on the one hand, that 'Plato says in the *Timaeus* that *hyle* and *chora* are the same thing' and, on the other, that 'in the so-called unwritten teachings' (*en tois legomenois agraphois dogmasin*) he called *chora* the 'participant' (*metaleptikon*) and identified it 'with the dyad great-small or with matter'. So uncritically is this testimony accepted (which may not astonish us when it comes to ancient commentators, but is, to say the least, surprising among the moderns) that the unwritten teachings are cited as though they were a work entitled *De bono*.[22] Moreover, the question is raised whether the term *hyle* already circulated in the Academy (from the lips of Speusippus rather than the master) or whether it is an Aristotelean invention, without noticing that the equivalence between the two concepts is thereby taken for granted. Under these conditions, it is difficult not to adopt Harold Cherniss's warning, according to which, given that Aristotle conveys the doctrines of the *Timaeus* arbitrarily (that *hyle* and *chora* are the same thing is said nowhere in the dialogue), his testimony on the unwritten doctrines might be just as untrustworthy.

Since the assertions contained in the commentaries on the *Physics* by Simplicius and John Philoponus repeat Aristotle's theses, perhaps the only one that should be carefully attended to is the one by Hermodorus, a companion of Plato (*tou Platonos etairou*) who Simplicius cites from the book by Dercyllides on

---

22 See Heinz Happ, *Hyle: Studien zum aristotelischen Materie-Begriff* (Berlin and New York: De Gruyter, 1971).

the philosophy of Plato. But here too we need to distinguish between Dercyllides' preamble—which affirms that Plato explained *hyle* on the basis of things that allow for more and less—from the words of Hermodorus himself, who does not explicitly cite the *Timaeus* but limits himself to contrasting entities said to be for themselves (*kath'auta*), which are immobile and stable, from those that are said to be with regard to others (*pros hetera*), and which always imply the more and the less, as well as contrariety. But even the final passage from Hermodorus—who uses terms like amorphous or unstable that could refer to *chora*—nevertheless affirms, in words whose Aristotelian derivation is evident, that *chora* is 'said not to be according to the negation of being'.[23]

The same can be said about the passage from Theophrastus' *Metaphysics*, in which we read that Plato and the Pythagoreans accept a kind of antithesis between the one and the unlimited dyad, in which we find 'the unlimited, the disordered and, so to speak, every absence of form [*to apeiron kai to atakton kai pasa os eipein amorphia*]', adding that without it not only 'would the nature of the whole not be possible' but that it has 'equal if not superior dignity to the One'.[24] In a reading of the *Timaeus*, it is certainly legitimate to keep this passage in consideration, but only on condition we do not to mix up the exegesis it contains with Plato's own words.

---

23 Simplicius, *Simplicii in Aristotelis Physicorum libros quattuor priores commentaria*, VOL. 1 (Hermann Diels ed.) (Berlin: G. Reimeri, 1882), pp. 247-48; Simplicius, *On Aristotle Physics 1.5-9* (Hans Baltussen, Michael Atkinson, Michael Share and Ian Mueller trans), Ancient Commentators on Aristotle (Richard Sorabji series ed.) (London: Bloomsbury, 2014), p. 132 [translation modified].

24 Theophrastus, *Métaphysique* (André Laks and Glenn W. Most eds and trans) (Paris: Les Belles Lettres, 1993), pp. 21-22.

3. In an amply documented study, Jean-François Pradeau has analysed the difference between the terms *chora* and *topos* in Greek, particularly in Plato's usage. In Greek, *chora* means above all 'the space that a thing occupies and which it frees up by moving' but also 'the territory of a political community, the region environing a city and whose lands are inhabited and cultivated.'[25] We should not to forget this double meaning—at once geographic and political—if we wish to understand the function of the term in the *Timaeus*, where it appears 12 times, as well as its difference with respect to *topos* (31 instances). As Pradeau observes:

> *Topos* always designates the place [*lieu*] in which a body finds itself or where it is situated. And the place is indissociable from the constitution of the body, which is to say also from its movement. But when Plato explains that every sensible reality possesses by definition a place, a proper place in which it carries out its function and conserves its nature, then he uses the term *chora*. From *topos* to *chora* we thus move from explanation and physical description to the postulation and definition of sensible reality. The use of the term becomes indispensable when Plato formulates his theory of

---

25 Jean-François Pradeau, 'Être quelque part, occupier une place: ΤΟΠΟΣ et ΧΩΡΑ dans le *Timée*', *Les Études philosophiques* 3 (1995): 375–400; here, p. 375.

relative places. This leads him to distinguish, among all places, proper places, those which conform with the elementary nature of the bodies in question; this only makes sense if we insert into the very definition of the sensible thing and the body the necessity of being somewhere (to possess a 'spot' [*place*]). In this way, one distinguishes the relative physical place from the ontological property that grounds this localization. To express this necessary localization, Plato resorts to the term *chora*, which designates the belonging to a subject of a limited and defined extension (whether we are dealing with the territory of the city or the place of a thing). Just as a city possesses a territory, so each body by definition has a certain spot, which is the one in which it carries out its function in accordance with its nature.[26]

What is particularly significant is the fact that *chora* is often associated with a verb that means 'possessing, holding, dominating', and is accordingly opposed to simple localization, as in 52b4: 'it is necessary that what exists is somewhere [*pou*] and in some place [*en tini topoi*] and possesses a certain *chora* [*katechon choran tiva*, its proper space or territory].' The difference between *topos* and *chora* is again underscored in the passage from the *Laws* we

---

26 Pradeau, 'Être quelque part, occupier une place': 396.

already cited and which curiously Pradeau does not examine: *ho topos emin tes choras*, or: 'the geographic localization
of the territory to which we belong.' Hence Pradeau's
further conclusion:

> This specification suffices to explain the meaning
> of the term *chora* in the *Timaeus* and offers the
> key to the distinction that Plato makes between
> *topos* and *chorai*, above all in its geographic and
> political aspects, when the region-*topos* (for
> example, a determinate city in a region with a tem-
> perate climate) is situated, when it is distinguished
> from the territory-*chora* possessed by a particular
> city (*Chora* then designates possession and par-
> ticularity, the proper territory of this city).
> Furthermore, in the domain of physics, of the
> description of the movement and localization of
> bodies, Plato distinguishes the different places in
> which a body may find itself according to its move-
> ment, from the place that a body occupies, its
> proper place.[27]

Summing up and further specifying Pradeau's considerations on the distinction between the two concepts, we
can inventory them in these paradigmatic oppositions:
localization/territoriality; geographic individuation/politi-
cal belonging; topographic reality/existential reality.

---

27 Pradeau, 'Être quelque part, occupier une place': 393.

4. Where Pradeau perhaps gest closest to a philosophical definition of *chora* is where he distinguishes it, as the 'ontological property that grounds localization', from *topos*, 'relative physical place'. It is undeniable, however, that it is not possible fully to grasp the philosophical meaning of the antinomy if one has not already tackled the other feature through which Plato—having already distinguished *chora*, as it were, *a parte objecti* from the other two principles, the intelligible and the sensible—tries to define it with respect to them in terms of the mode of its knowability. After having specified that the first kind—the 'immutable, ungenerated and immortal' intelligible—is insensible (*anaistheton*) and can only be known in thought, while the second, the sensible, 'generated and always in movement', can be perceived *met'aistheseos*, in sensation, Plato affirms that the third kind 'can be attained with a bastard kind of reasoning [*logismoi tini nothoi*] with the absence of sensation [*met'anaisthesias*]' (52b2). While all the interpreters have dwelled on the 'bastard kind of reasoning', which is such because it is neither intelligible nor sensible, the second expression—which had elicited Calcidius' amazement—has generally remained unaddressed. Among the moderns, only Carlo Diano has noted the paradoxical character of the formulation *met'anaisthesias*, 'accompanied by an absence of sensation', and has rightly asked why Plato wrote 'with the absence of sensation' and not simply

'without sensation, *koris aistheseos*'.[28] Calcidius' translation *sine sensu*, followed by almost all the moderns, is misleading because it flattens the third kind onto the first, which is obviously impossible.

What we are dealing with, therefore, are three modalities of knowledge, to each of which corresponds a particular kind of being. The three modalities of knowledge form a system: while the object of the first kind is not perceivable by the senses—it is *anaistheton*, not sensible—and the second is perceived instead *met'aistheseos*, with sensation, *chora* compresses together the other two modes of knowledge and is perceived, so to speak, with an absence of sensation, through an anaesthesia (in the words of Diano, 'with the sense of this absence').[29] This is possible only if sensation feels itself as lacking an object, only, that is, through an auto-affection. Sensation here is neither devoid of an object (as in the first non-sensible kind) nor does it have a sensible object, as in the second kind; rather, perceiving itself as lacking a sensible external object, it perceives, so to speak, its own anaesthesia. The knowledge of *chora* is of a bastard kind, because it experiences neither an intelligible reality nor a sensible object, but its own receptivity; it suffers its own anaesthesia. In perceiving an objectless receptivity, it knows a pure power of knowing, a pure knowability.

---

28 Carlo Diano, *Studi e saggi di filosofia antica* (Padua: Antenore, 1973), p. 272.

29 Diano, *Studi e saggi di filosofia antica*, p. 179.

Diano rightly links the Platonic *chora* (which he calls matter)[30] to the being-there of phenomenology, to the very structure of Dasein. We should reread in this key the pages where Heidegger, in *Being and Time*, defines the spatiality proper to Dasein. Being-there is not in space, nor is space, as in Kant, an *a priori* form of its inner sense; being-there, in whose being being itself is at stake, is always already spatial; spatiality constitutively belongs to it.

> *Space is not in the subject, nor is the world in space.* Space is rather 'in' the world in so far as space has been disclosed by that Being-in-the-world which is constitutive for Dasein. Space is not to be found in the subject, nor does the subject observe the world 'as if' that world were in a space; but the 'subject' (Dasein), if well understood ontologically, is spatial. And because Dasein is spatial in the way we have described, space shows itself as *a priori*.[31]

If space appears as constitutive of the world, this is because 'Dasein's own spatiality is essential to its basic state of Being-in-the-world,'[32] which coincides with the very opening of Dasein. From this perspective, it is clear why at the end of his philosophical journey, Heidegger could declare that *Being and Time*'s attempt to reduce space to temporality had to be abandoned. The insistence of the final writings on the theme of the Open and *Lichtung* (the clearing) is a coherent reprise of the originary spatiality of being-there.

---

30 Diano, *Studi e saggi di filosofia antica*, p. 178.
31 Heidegger, *Being and Time*, p. 146.
32 Heidegger, *Being and Time*, p. 148.

5. We can now understand why Plato took care to distinguish spatiality from matter and from the place strictly understood. What is at stake, in *chora*, is not that things are constituted by a *hyle*, by a certain construction material, nor that they are in a precise place, but, so to speak, that they 'take place', in the sense of 'existing', 'happening and being manifest'. The etymology of the Latin term *spatium*, from *patere*, being open and extended, is instructive in this regard. What is in a certain place (*en topi tini*) thereby has its own spatiality and extension—provided we understand extension not as Descartes' *res extensa* nor as the Aristotelian *hypokeimenon* but as an opening and extension in the etymological sense (a tension towards the outside) distinct from the body that nevertheless occupies it. *Chora* is the opening, the *spatium*, the 'spacing' [*spaziatura*] or knowability that pertains to something insofar as it exists and takes place. It is not the gold whereof the object is made, but its pure being-in-gold, its emplacement [*indovarsi*] as distinct from its place [*dove*]. We should distinguish, in this sense, being-in from that in which something is. The *hypodoke* is not the receptacle but receptivity, the hospitality wherein each body necessarily opens itself and lives, both mother and wet nurse, at once passive and active.

Here the closeness between *chora* and matter becomes especially significant, while their difference is also illuminated. *Chora* is not a substance nor, like matter in Aristotle, a quasi-substance (*Physics* 192a: 'close to and in some way *ousia*'): it is what allows for the givenness and modification (in the Spinozist sense) of forms in sensible bodies, their spacing and knowability. Matter and *chora* communicate in receptivity and being-in, but they are distinguished from these because *chora* is, as it were, always tensed towards an outside, while matter in Aristotle is what subtends and lies beneath. But if we were to understand matter too as a tension, as a materialization [*materiarsi*] and taking place, if we introduced into it—as Aristotle tried to do through the concept of privation (*steresis*)—a tension towards form and existence, then the distance between the two concepts would undoubtedly be lessened.

6. The theory of *chora* emerges in the late Plato to resolve the aporias of the relation between ideas and sensible things, as a brilliant riposte to the contradictions produced by the *chorismos*, by the drastic separation between the intelligible and the sensible. A Japanese philosopher, Norio Fujisawa, has sought to show how the language of participation (*methexis, metechein, metalepsis, metalambanein*) used to explain the relation between ideas and the sensible only appears in the middle dialogues, beginning with the *Symposium*, and disappears in the final dialogues, to be replaced by the language of the paradigm, already present from the start.[33] The critique of participation undertaken

---

33 Norio Fujisawa, '"Εχειν, Μετέχειν, and Idioms of "Paradeigmatism"' in Plato's Theory of Forms', *Phronesis* 19 (1974): 30–57.

in the *Parmenides* (131a–134a) is in keeping with the critique of the separate existence of ideas and sensible things, while in the final dialogues the paradigm makes it possible to formulate the relation between the intelligible and the sensible without recourse to any idea of participation. Against the thesis, advanced by numerous scholars, according to which, given that the language of participation implies immanence and that of the paradigm implies transcendence, Plato's thought would undergo a decided shift from an immanent to a transcendent model, Fujisawa can comfortably demonstrate that participation on the contrary implies transcendence[34] and that, if anything, the trajectory of Platonic thought goes in the inverse direction. Even though Fujisawa drops the problem, we should at least recall here that the term *paradeigma* does not mean archetype or model, but above all 'example', and that the example (literally, what is shown besides) is certainly not transcendent with respect to the things that follow or imitate it.

The fact is, however, that at least in the *Timaeus*, which particularly concerns us here, it is not so much a question, *pace* Fujisawa, of playing off the paradigm against participation. If already in the *Parmenides* (132d) even the idea of the paradigm appears to lead to contradictions, in the *Timaeus* both idioms are present (about the *chora* it is said that it participates in the intelligible—*metalambanon . . . tou noetou*; 51b), but it's a question of resolving the drastic

34 Fujisawa, '"Εχειν, Μετέχειν, and Idioms of "Paradeigmatism"': 47.

opposition between transcendence and immanence through the idea of a *chora*, of a 'taking place' together of ideas and sensible entities.

Pronouncing the discourse on *chora* to be a new beginning, Timaeus clearly says that it has been rendered necessary by the insufficiency of the antinomic division between intelligible and sensible:

> The earlier two kinds sufficed [*ikana*] for our previous account: one was proposed as a paradigm, intelligible and always changeless, a second as an imitation of the paradigm, something that possesses becoming and is visible. We did not distinguish a third kind at the time, because we thought that we could make do with the two of them [*exein ikanos*]. Now, however, it appears that our account compels us to attempt to illuminate in words a kind that is difficult and vague.[35]

It is only thanks to this third kind that we 'perceive dreaming' how sensible things, 'always borne along as phantasms of something else', can exist and take place (52c) and how, on the other hand, ideas can impress their image on them 'in a marvelous way that is hard to describe [*dysphraston kai thaumaston*]'.[36]

---

35 Plato, *Timaeus* (Zeyl trans.), pp. 37–38 (48e–49a) [translation modified].

36 Plato, *Timaeus* (Zeyl trans.), p. 39 (50c).

In this sense, the Derridean interpretation of *chora* as a sort of pre-origin 'before the "world", before creation, before the gift and being'[37] can seem pertinent, with the proviso that here there can be no before, because *chora*, like every true origin, results only from the neutralization of the two other principles that are coeval with it ('the three principles in three modes [*tria triche*]' exist 'before the heavens').[38] This is what Plato suggests when he writes that as long as two things are kept separate, 'neither of them ever comes to be in the other in such a way that they at the same time become one thing and also two'.[39] In the *chora*, the intelligible and the sensible are indeed one thing and also two.

To show how two things can be 'one thing and also two', Plato employs the image of the letter *chi*. At the end of the description of the creation of the soul, Timaeus explains that, having sculpted the form of the soul according to complicated numerical relations, the deity

> sliced this entire compound in two along its length, joined the two halves together center to center like the letter *chi* [*oion khei*], and bent them back in a circle, attaching each half to itself end to end and to the

---

37 Jacques Derrida, *Rogues: Two Essays on Reason* (Pascale-Anne Brault and Michael Naas trans) (Stanford, CA: Stanford University Press, 2005), p. xv.

38 Plato, *Timaeus* (Zeyl trans.), p. 42 (52d) [translation modified].

39 Plato, *Timaeus* (Zeyl trans.), p. 42 (52d) [translation modified].

ends of the other half at the point opposite to their intersection.[40]

Just as in this manner the same and the other are united and at the same time separated in the structure of the soul, so the third kind unites and at the same time divides the intelligible and the sensible. In the *chora* that offers a common place and homeland for the two principles, we should perceive, as would have been inevitable for a Greek ear, a reference and riposte to their division (*chorismos*). The *chora* in this sense has the structure of a chiasmus.

7. Here we must thoroughly rethink the specific meaning of 'being-in' that defines *chora*. In a passage from Book 4 of the *Physics*, concerning the problem of the place, Aristotle reflects on the expression 'being-in', asking himself 'in how many ways one thing is said to be *in* another [*pos allo en alloi legetai*]'. After having evoked the part and the whole ('In one way, as the finger is in the hand, and, generally, the part in the whole'), and the species and genus ('as man is in animal'), he mentions as a more general (*olos*) meaning form and matter ('as the form is in the matter [*to eidos en tei hyle*]'), to then define as the most proper (*panton kyriotaton*) meaning of all the strictly locational one ('as [a thing is] in a vessel and, generally, in a

---

40 Plato, *Timaeus* (Zeyl trans.), p. 21 (36b-c) [translation modified]. [The letter *chi* in the Greek alphabet is written 'X'.]

place [*en topoi*]').⁴¹ This passage comes shortly after the one we have repeatedly cited, where Aristotle asserts that Plato had mistakenly identified matter with *chora* (209b11).

While Aristotle clearly seems intent on privileging the locational meaning of being-in against the supposed Platonic identification of space and matter, what we need to understand is the meaning of being-in within the strategy of the *Timaeus*. If the separation between the intelligible and the sensible appears insufficient here (just as it already led to unacceptable consequences in the *Parmenides*), the third kind allows for a resolution of the antinomy by offering the intelligible and the sensible a space where to be-in together.

At the point where we perceive neither the sensible nor the intelligible but, thanks to a 'bastard kind of reasoning accompanied by an absence of sensation [*met'anaisthesias*]', their taking place, their emplacement and being in one another, then the intelligible and the sensible in some way coincide, they fall together. What comes to be known here is not an object but pure knowability. This is why Plato can write that *chora*, 'a kind of invisible species devoid of form [*anoraton eidos ti kai amorphon*]', insofar as it receives into itself the species of the sensible, 'participates in the intelligible in the most impassable [*aporotata*] and impregnable [*dysalototaton*] manner'.⁴²

---

41 Aristotle, *Physics: Books III and IV*, p. 24 (210a14–24).
42 Plato, *Timaeus* (Zeyl trans.), p. 40 (51a–b) [translation modified].

It is the manner of this participation, no matter how 'impassable and impregnable' that we need to interrogate. Once again, the key is the modality of knowledge 'with absence of sensation'. The perception of an anaesthesia, the touching with an absence of sensation is an inchoative act of thought or, more precisely, a threshold—whence the 'impassable'—in which the passage from sensation to intelligence occurs; in this sense, it is no longer sensation and not yet thought. Analogously, Pierre Duhem, in the section of his *Système du monde* dedicated to the Platonic theory of space, has shown that the 'bastard kind of reasoning' at stake in the *Timaeus* is nothing but 'geometric reasoning, which is grounded as much on *noesis* as—through the imagination that accompanies it—on *aesthesis*'.[43] Elementary geometric figures, which the *Timaeus* connects to each of the elements (the *kybikon eidos* to earth, and so forth) are in fact both ideal and sensible and, as Rivaud suggests, it is in them 'that occurs the passage from the ideal to the sensible order, and participation takes place'.[44] While Plato warns repeatedly about the difficulty of his exposition, this does not mean he is shunting the theory of the *chora* into the ineffable, for he knows he is addressing readers familiar with 'inquiry by means of rational argument'[45] and capable

---

43 Pierre Duhem, *Système du monde: Histoire des doctrines cosmologiques de Platon à Copernic*, vol. I (Paris: Hermann, 1913), p. 37.

44 Albert Rivaud, Introduction to Plato, *Timée, Critias* (Paris: Les Belles Lettres, 1963), p. 72.

45 Plato, *Timaeus* (Zeyl trans.), p. 40 (51c).

of following him on the impassable path into which he is leading them.

Intelligible and sensible, separate and non-communicating are two necessary abstractions, which only *chora* allows one to think together. *Chora* offers a 'where' to the two first principles but, within it, these fall away and what remains in the end is a pure knowability, a pure exteriority. Here we need to restore to paradigm its meaning as example, that which shows itself besides (*para-deigma*) and makes knowable: being-in is not simply a relation between intelligible and sensible, it is what grants them knowability. Paradigmaticity, which holds the idea and the sensible thing together in *chora*, is a pure mediality, through which the intelligible may be touched with anaesthesia and the sensible thought with a bastard reasoning. And it is this mediality, this pure knowability—and not an object, be it intelligible or sensible—that is at stake in *chora*.

In her dense book *On the Diaphanous*, Anca Vasiliu has forcefully underscored the mediality that defines *chora*: 'The third kind (that is to say, that in which something becomes, *to d'en hoi gignetai*) is in a median position with regard to the other two kinds: what becomes (*to men gignomenon*) and that resembling which what becomes is born (*to d'othen aphomoioumenon phyetai to gignomenon*).'[46] The median position of the third kind corresponds

---

46 Anca Vasiliu, *Du diaphane: Image, milieu, lumière dans la pensée antique et médiévale* (Paris: Vrin, 1997).

to the definition of the middle term in a proportion, which Timaeus invoked with regard to the elements: 'But it isn't possible to combine two things well all by themselves, without a third [*tritou koris*]; there has to be some bond [*desmon*] between [*en mesoi*] the two that united them'.[47]

Truth be told, a good definition of Plato's thought, by contrast with a widespread representation of it that exaggerates its antinomic structure, would be one that characterizes it in terms of the essential function played within it by the concept of medium (*metaxy*). In the *Symposium* as in the *Timaeus*, the antinomies with which Plato begins come to be composed in a mediality. The theory of *chora* is the euphoria in which Plato dissolves the aporias of the *Parmenides*.

This is the perspective from which we must understand the absence of form that for Plato defines *chora*. If what received all forms had some form in itself, it could not receive them, because it would unavoidably show its form alongside the other (*ten autou paremphainon opsin*). But Plato does not limit himself to characterizing *chora* as amorphous (it is an *eidos anoraton kai amorphon*; 51a); he specifies that it is 'outside all forms [*panton ektos eidon*]' (50e). The same singular expression is forcefully reprised shortly thereafter: 'it ought to be by nature outside all forms [*panton ektos auto prosekei pephykenai ton eidon*]' (51a). *Ektos*, opposed to *entos* (within), indicates what is outside,

---

47 Plato, *Timaeus* (Zeyl trans.), p. 17 (31b).

exterior: *ta ektos* are external things (*oi ektos*, those from outside, namely, foreigners). *Chora* is not amorphous like a raw material but like a pure exteriority, a pure outside: it is the outside, the exteriority of forms, their pure taking place. This is what Plotinus intuits when he compares matter and *chora* to a mirror:

> hence the things which seem to come to be in it are frivolities, nothing but phantoms in a phantom [*eidola en eidoloi*], like something in a mirror which really exists in one place but is reflected in another; it seems to be filled, and holds nothing; it is all seeming. 'Imitations of real beings pass into and out of it', ghosts into a formless ghost, visible because of its formlessness.[48]

8. In the summer semester of 1944, when Germany's defeat already seemed inevitable and Hitler, on July 20, had miraculously survived an assassination attempt organized by officers of the Wehrmacht, Heidegger taught a course on Heraclitus, whose title reads: *Logic: Heraclitus' Doctrine of the Logos*. What is at stake in it is the reconstruction of the Heraclitean conception of Logos by way of the reading and commentary of a series of fragments. Having reached fragment 108, which is usually translated as 'of all whose discourses I have heard, there is not one who succeeds in understanding that the wise man is apart from all [*oti sophon esti panton kechorismenon*],' he renders these final

---

words in an altogether new way: 'the proper to-be-known, in relation to all beings, unfolds from out of its (own) region [*im Bezug auf alles seiende aus seiner (eigenen) Gegend west*].'[49] He justifies this unprecedented translation of the term *kechorismenon* by relating it to the term *chora*:

> It is not necessary for us to impose upon the decisive word κεχωρισμένον a meaning thought up specifically for it. It is only necessary that we keep the word free of the meaning that is conventionally, tritely, and superficially ascribed to it, and allow it to retain the dignity of a word spoken by a thinker in order to name what is properly to-be-known. κεχωρισμένον belongs to χωρίζω/χωρίζειν, which one translates as 'cutting-off,' 'separating,' and 'moving-away.' Given these words, one only thinks of the moving away of one thing from another [*wegstellen*], thereby paying attention neither to what belongs to moving away and what lies at its foundation, nor to the fact that in the translation as 'separating' and 'cutting off' one hears not the faintest glimmer of the Greek word's meaning. [. . .] In the verb χωρίζειν lies ἡ χώρα, ὁ χῶρος, which we translate as: surroundings [*die Umgebung*, that which is given around, G. A.], surroundings that

49 Martin Heidegger, *Heraclitus: The Inception of Occidental Thinking / Logic: Heraclitus' Doctrine of the Logos* (Julia Goesser Assaiante and S. Montgomery Ewegen trans) (London: Bloomsbury, 2018), p. 247.

enclose [*die umgebende Umgegend*], that make
room for and guarantee a sojourning. The nouns
χώρα/χῶρος trace back to χάω (from which χάος
is derived): 'yawning,' 'gaping,' 'opening up,' 'self-
opening'; ἡ χώρα as the surroundings that surround is then 'the region.' We understand this to
be the open area and the expanse [*den offenen
Bereich und die Weite*] in which something takes
its sojourn, wherefrom it arrives, escapes, and
responds. ἡ χώρα, as the region, can also be named,
in an imprecise manner of speaking, 'the place.'
However, 'region' and 'place' are not the same. For
'place,' the Greeks have the word τόπος.[50]

At this juncture, Heidegger attempts, not without difficulty,
to define the meaning of *chora*-region with respect to *topos*-
place. The region (*Gegend*) is not the place, 'but rather that
surrounding, self-opening and forth-coming expanse that
grants places and directions [*die umgebende, Orte und
Richtungen gewährende, sich öffnende und entgegenkom-
mende Weite*].'[51] Insofar as it

always surrounds places and grants them and
thereby first allows the founding and occupation
of places, it is, from a certain perspective, the essential feature of a place, its locality [*Ortschaft*]. This

---

50 Heidegger, *Heraclitus*, pp. 249–50.
51 Heidegger, *Heraclitus*, p. 250.

and only this is the reason that χώρα can also mean place in the sense of a site that has been occupied [*der eingenommene Platz*], a region that is claimed [*in Anspruch genommenen Gegend*] in accordance with particular measurements and demarcations.⁵²

And it is in places that the force which 'joins and shapes [*das Fügende und Prägende*]' appears in full light, without ever itself becoming an object. 'The objectlessness of the region [*das Gegenstandlose der Gegend*] is the sign of its superior, and not inferior, being.'⁵³ The comprehension of the verb *khorizein* on the basis of *chora*, Heidegger concludes, is therefore 'neither an exaggerated demand, nor something violent',⁵⁴ because it means 'to bring into surroundings that surround, into a region, and from out of this region to allow to presence.'⁵⁵

The insistence, on the basis of the term *chora*, on the non-arbitrariness of the understanding of a verb that means 'to separate', betrays a difficulty, which concerns how a thinking of being articulates itself in a decidedly spatial terminology. In other words, it is possible to discern in what seems to be merely the interpretation of a Heraclitean fragment the symptom of that shifting of ontological

52 Heidegger, *Heraclitus*, p. 250 [translation modified].

53 Heidegger, *Heraclitus*, p. 250.

54 Heidegger, *Heraclitus*, p. 250.

55 Heidegger, *Heraclitus*, p. 250.

conceptuality from the temporal to the spatial sphere that defines Heidegger's final thinking.

In a text from nine years prior, almost entirely devoted to the comprehension of the verb 'to be', the difficulty of seizing the ontological meaning of spatial terms is announced in a passage that features the first appearance of the term *chora* in Heidegger's thought. In the chapter 'On the Grammar and Etymology of the Word "Being"', he writes:

> That within which something becomes is what we call space [*Raum*]. The Greeks have no word for space. This is no accident, for they do not experience the spatial according to *nergeia* but instead according to place (*topos*) as *chora*, which means neither place nor space but what is taken up and occupied by what stands there. The place belongs to the thing itself. [. . .] That which becomes is set into this local space and Is set forth from it.[56]

At this point, Heidegger quotes the passage from the *Timaeus* on how *chora* is necessarily devoid of its own form and immediately adds some parenthetical considerations that we would do well to reflect on:

> The reference to the *Timaeus* passage not only intends to clarify the correlation of *paremphainon*

---

56 Martin Heidegger, *Introduction to Metaphysics* (Gregory Fried and Richard Polt trans) (New Haven, CT: Yale University Press, 2000), p. 69 [translation modified].

CHORA · 197

and *on*, of appearing-with and of Being as constancy, but also tries to intimate that Platonic philosophy—that is, the interpretation of Being as *idea*—prepared the transfiguration of place (*topos*) and of *chora*, the essence of which we have barely grasped, into 'space' as defined by extension. Might not *chora mean*: that which separates itself from every particular, that which withdraws, and in this way admits and 'makes room' precisely for something else?[57]

The inflection of a 'barely grasped [*kaum gefast*]' thinking of place and *chora* in the direction of extension,[58] which is here curiously imputed precisely to the philosopher which had first theorized it, once again betrays a difficulty that Heidegger himself will repeatedly be obliged to confront. If it is true that Heidegger's final thinking can be defined as the attempt to shift the thought of being from time to space, it is equally true that in this effort he seems to come up against difficulties which he was not able to dispel. And it is possible, as some have suggested,[59] that these difficulties were rooted in an insufficient engagement with the *chora* of the *Timaeus*.

---

57 Heidegger, *Introduction to Metaphysics*, p. 70.

58 The allusion is in all likelihood to the doctrine of *res extensa* that Descartes would have bequeathed to modernity.

59 Nader El-Bizri, 'On ΚΑΙ ΧΩΡΑ: Situating Heidegger Between the *Sophist* and the *Timaeus*', *Studia Phaenomenologica* 4(1–2) (2004): 73–98.

198 · GIORGIO AGAMBEN

In *Zur sache des Denkens* (*On Time and Being*), Heidegger unreservedly asserts that the attempt in §70 of *Being and Time* to lead space back to temporality cannot be sustained. In a similarly emphatic way, in *Four Seminars*, he reminds the reader that his thinking no longer interrogates the meaning of being, but being's place and locality.[60] However, as attested by the febrile annotations on time-space (*Zeitraum*) in the section 'Time-Space as the Abyssal Ground' of the *Contributions to Philosophy*, the concept of time is never abandoned.[61] Thus, in the dialogue 'To Indicate the Place of Abandonment' in *Gelassenheit*,[62] the concept of region is forcefully reprised, though it is defined with a play on words as the crossing of a spatial concept (*Weite*, vastness or expanse) and a temporal concept (*Weile*, duration). The region, time-space, *Ereignis*—in the final analysis, these are concepts through which Heidegger still tries to name a figure of being. As Reiner Schürmann has shown, the final Heidegger abandons being as the principle of epochal-historical sendings but not being as pure coming to presence.[63] It is therefore not surprising that the evocation of *chora* in the 1944 course on Heraclitus concludes with the identification between the region-*chora* and

---

60 Martin Heidegger, *Four Seminars* (Andrew J. Mitchell and François Raffoul trans) (Bloomington, IN: Indiana University Press, 2003).

61 Martin Heidegger, *Contributions to Philosophy* (*Of the Event*) (Richard Rojcewicz and Daniela Vallega-Neu trans) (Bloomington, IN: Indiana University Press, 2012).

62 Martin Heidegger, *Discourse on Thinking: A Translation of Gelassenheit* (John M. Anderson and E. Hans Freund trans) (New York: Harper & Row, 1966).

63 Reiner Schürmann, *Heidegger on Being and Acting: From Principles to Anarchy* (Christine-Marie Gros trans.) (Bloomington, IN: Indiana University Press, 1990).

logos: 'The Λόγος is, as λόγος, πάντων κεχωρισμένον: it is the all-surrounding region which, in relation to the whole of beings, is open for all and counters all [*und allem sich entgegnende*].'[64] Here Heidegger tries to think the relation between region-logos and being and, in this sense, tries to exit ontology in the direction of a chorology.

9. The time has come to interrogate anew the modalities of the existence and knowability of *chora*, which Timaeus, as we saw, defines as 'impassable and impregnable', such that they can only be grasped through a bastard kind of reasoning accompanied by the absence of sensation. In the *Republic*—the dialogue whose contiguity with the *Timaeus* is discretely evoked by Socrates with a 'yesterday' ('I talked about politics yesterday')[65]—Plato, having compared the idea of the good to the sun, which grants visibility to things seen, employs the term *chora* in a decisive passage of the myth of the cave. The one who, having wrenched himself from the shadows of the cave, has finally climbed back up towards the sun, will at first perforce be blinded by the radiance but then, slowly becoming accustomed to the light, 'he'd be able to see the sun, not images of it in water or another medium, but the sun itself, in its own place [*en tei autou chora*], and be able to contemplate it.'[66]

---

64 Heidegger, *Heraclitus*, p. 252 [translation modified].

65 Plato, *Timaeus* (Zeyl trans.), p. 1 (17b).

It is worth reflecting on the proximity that Plato thereby introduces between *chora* and the idea of the good, whose symbol is the sun. There is a *chora* of the good and the loftiest moment is the one in which we finally contemplate the idea of the good in its *chora*, its region and its proper knowability. Shortly before, in a passage that has been commented upon countless times (509b6–9), it is said of the good that it confers upon known things not only knowability but also being and *ousia* and that it is 'beyond being' (*epekeina tes ousias*). What does it mean that the good is beyond being? Like the idea of the good, *chora* too is not a thing—a substrate or a matter according to Aristotle's misunderstanding—but what grants things their knowability. The *megiston mathema*, the greatest knowledge, is not the cognition of a thing, but of a knowability. This does not mean that it sinks into a mystical fog but that, like *chora*, it is a pure outwardness or exteriority, a being outside all forms of the cave and the world, not in another place, but in their very manifesting and taking place.

If the ultimate problem of Platonism can be stated in the question 'How do things exist that are beyond being, how are those things that are-not-there [*ci-non-sono*]?', a possible answer is that these coincide with the knowability of the things that are there. Again, *chora* is what grants this knowability, and to see the sun, the idea of the good,

66 Plato, *Republic*, p. 1134 (516c) [translation modified].

in its *chora* means contemplating it in its taking place 'neither in heaven or earth', but in the nergeias and knowability of every entity.

It is truly remarkable that, as John Sallis observes,[67] Derrida held that there was no relationship between the *chora* of the *Republic* and the *chora* of the *Timaeus*. Sallis suggests instead that not only is there a relationship, but that *chora* could also be connected with the beyond of being that Derrida repeatedly invoked in his writings on *Chora*.

10. 'One, two, three . . . Where's number four, Timaeus? The four of you were my guests yesterday and today I'm to be yours.'[68] Faced with this highly unusual opening of the dialogue, which begins by noting an absence, scholars and commentators have above all tried to identify the missing fourth guest. Dercyllides, according to Proclus' testimony, already identified the absent fourth with Plato himself.[69] Giuseppe Fraccaroli, in his edition of the dialogue in the

---

67 John Sallis, 'Last Words: Generosity and Reserve', *Mosaic* 39(3) (2006): 20–22.

68 Plato, *Timaeus* (Zeyl trans.), p. 1 (17a).

69 Proclus, *Commentary on Plato's 'Timaeus', Volume I, Book 1: Proclus on the Socratic State and Atlantis* (Harold Tarrant ed. and trans.) (Cambridge: Cambridge University Press, 2010), p. 144.

first volume of the collection *Il pensiero nerg* (1906) by the Fratelli Bocca publishing house, follows, like Rivaud, Dercyllides' opinion, and supports it by invoking the analogous absence of Plato from the *Phaedo* by reason of illness ('Plato was, I believe, sick [*esthenei*]'). Others, instead, beginning with Constantin Ritter,[70] think that Plato intended to compose a tetraology and that the absent fourth was actually the dialogue he intended to write after the *Timaeus*, *Critias* and *Hermocrates* (also never written). It is noteworthy that as acute a scholar as Paul Friedländer could also hazard an analogous hypothesis, given it implies that we take on board the attribution that Thrasyllus refers back to Plato himself, regarding the latter's decision to publish the dialogues in the form of tetralogies.

Among efforts to identify the fourth guest as a historical figure, perhaps the most persuasive is the one contained in the resolutely political reading of the dialogue proposed by Laurence Lampert and Christopher Planeaux.[71] According to them, in these dialogues Plato puts cosmology in the service of politics and consequently proposes a new theological-political scenario to replace the Homeric one. That is why the guests are the statesmen involved in Greece's recent history: Timaeus, as the repre-

---

70 Constantin Ritter, 'Timaios cap. I', *Philologus* 62(1) (1903): 410–18.

71 Laurence Lampert and Christopher Planeaux, 'Who's Who in Plato's *Timaeus-Critias* and Why', *Review of Metaphysics* 52(1) (1998): 87–125.

sentative of Locris, a city which in 426 BCE allied itself with Syracuse against Athens and where, as Socrates informs us, 'he has come to occupy positions of supreme authority'; Critias of Athens ('no mere layman in any of the areas we're talking about'); and Hermocrates of Syracuse, who Thucydides described as 'second to none in intelligence', and profoundly engaged as a strategist in the victorious war against the Athenian invasion.[72] In this political context, the fourth guest can be none other, according to Lampert and Planeaux, than Alcibiades, namely, the protagonist of Athens' imperialist politics, both in the Peloponnesian and in the ill-starred expedition against Syracuse.[73] Like in the *Symposium*, which is set in 416 BCE, when the profanation of the mysteries took place that led to the accusation of impiety against Alcibiades, and the latter arrived too late to hear the guests' discourses on Eros, so in the *Timaeus* Alcibiades cannot be present for the argument that inaugurates a new and more just cosmological horizon for the city he will end up betraying. The *astheneia* that prevents him from attending is not an illness but, according to the term's more proper meaning, a moral weakness or infirmity.

---

72 Plato, *Timaeus* (Zeyl trans.), p. 5 (20a2).

73 Lampert and Planeaux, 'Who's Who in Plato's *Timaeus-Critias* and Why': 108.

It is beyond doubt that the *Timaeus*, like all of Plato's thought, has a political dimension; it is difficult, however, not to discern in the dialogue's opening something that refers not only to the political context, but also and above all to the substantive meaning of the philosophical doctrines it explores. While Proclus informs us that Syrianus already read into Socrates' words a nod to the esoteric meaning of the tetrad and the triad in Pythagoreanism, Calcidius, in his own commentary, writing about the three-dimensional geometrical solid as 'the principle underlying the union of soul and body,' does not fail to evoke the importance of the number series 1, 2, 3, 4 for the Pythagoreans, because their sum is the perfect number ten.[74] Closer to our own time, Carl Gustav Jung related the incipit of the *Timaeus* to his doctrine of the Quaternity as a fundamental psychological archetype.

Against the vagueness of such correlations, it is worth closely following the status of the numbers three and four, which incessantly recur in the dialogue precisely at those points where the philosophical density is highest and especially in the exposition of the doctrine of *chora*. We have already evoked the passage in which Timaeus, prefiguring the status of *chora*, expounds his theory of the proportional middle, which we can now read more attentively:

---

74 'The Pythagoreans refer to the number 10 as the primary square on the grounds that it is the composite of the first four numbers, 1, 2, 3, 4.' Calcidius, *On Plato's 'Timaeus'*, pp. 171, 175.

it isn't possible to combine two [elements] in a beautiful manner all by themselves, without a third; there has to be some bond between the two that unites them. Now the most beautiful bond is one that really and truly makes a unity of itself together with the things bonded by it, and this in the nature of things is best accomplished by analogy [*analogia*]. For whenever of three numbers (or bulks or powers) the middle term [*meson*] between any two of them is such that what the first term is to it, it is to the last, and, conversely, what the last term is to the middle, it is to the first, then, since the middle term turns out to be both first and last, and the last and the first likewise both turn out to be middle terms, they will all of necessity turn out to have the same relationship to each other, and, given this, will all become one [*hen panta estai*].[75]

If, through the mediation of the third, the first two terms— just as will happen in the *chora* for the intelligible and the sensible—become one thing, it follows that this *hen* will now be, with respect to the initial three, a fourth, albeit not named as such.

---

75 Plato, *Timaeus*, p. 17 (31b-32a) [translation modified].

Shortly thereafter, with reference to the creation of the soul, the same schema seems to repeat itself, with the difference that a fourth is explicitly evoked:

> From the mixture between the indivisible and always changeless essence, and the one that is divisible and comes to be in the corporeal realm, he created a third kind of being [*triton . . . ousias eidos*], intermediate between the other two [*ex amphoin en mesoi*], between the nature of the one and the other, and he put it in the middle between its indivisible and its corporeal, divisible counterparts. And he took the three mixtures and mixed them together to make a single form [*eis mian panta idean*].[76]

But it is in the exposition of the doctrine of the *chora* that the relation between the 'three in three forms [*tria triche*]' (52d) takes on its full meaning. If *chora* is the middle term that allows one somehow to hold together the intelligible and the sensible, it is obvious that from this union will issue a fourth that will remain unnamed, and which is the true figure of the cosmos once the antinomy has been resolved. The fourth that is in question here must not be understood according to a temporal succession nor simply as the opening of a locality. It does not imply a measurable chronology, nor does it resolve itself into an ecstatic kairology. And it is this fourth which perhaps, at the dialogue's

---

76 Plato, *Timaeus*, p. 19 (35a) [translation modified].

end, when 'the account of the whole has reached its end [*telos echein*]' and 'this cosmos has grasped together living mortals and immortals and attained fullness,' Plato evokes in the figure of a 'a perceptible god [*theos aisthetos*], image of the intelligible one, the greatest, most beautiful and perfect, a single monogenic heaven'.[77] The perceptible god is the sensible intelligible and the intelligible sensible, namely, the thing in the medium of its knowability: the sun—idea of the good—in its *chora*. True philosophy, like true politics, is a chorology.

The image of a perceptible god that closes the *Timaeus* is reprised in one of the most astounding texts in the history of philosophy: the fragment *Mens hyle deus* by David of Dinant:

> One sees that Plato agrees with this when he says that the world is a sensible God [*mundum esse Deum sensibilem*]. For the mind that we are describing and that we are calling singular and impassible is none other than God [*Mens enim de qua loquimur et quam unam dicimus esse eamquem impassibilem, nihil aliud est quam Deus*]. If the world is therefore God himself without his being accessible himself to sense, as Plato, Zeno, Socrates, and many others have said, then the matter of the world is God himself, and the form that comes to matter is none other than God making himself sensible [*Si ergo mundus est ipse Deus preter se ipsum perceptibile sensui, ut Plato et Zeno et Socrates et multi alii*

---

77 Plato, *Timaeus* (Zeyl trans.), p. 88 (92c) [translation modified].

*dixerunt, yle igitur mundi est ipse Deus, forma vero adve-
niens yle nil aliud quam id, quod facit Deus sensibile se
ipsum].*[78]

David is named alongside Amalric of Bena among the representatives of thirteenth-century pantheism. Amalric interpreted
Saint Paul's sentence according to which 'God is all in all' as a
radical theological elaboration of the Platonic doctrine of *chora*.
God is in each thing as the place in which each thing is. That is
why he could say, according to what his scandalized adversaries
report, that God is stone in the stone, and bat in the bat. David's
gesture differs but is akin to Amalric's in its ultimate outcome. If
the mind, which is one for all souls, comprehends matter which,
like the *chora*, is one for all bodies, that is because mind and
matter become one thing. Therefore, there is a single substance
and that substance is god, but a god which, like the cosmos of
the *Timaeus*, has thereby made itself sensible.

The message that Plato's final thought entrusted to *chora*
and that David brings to its most extreme formulation (once we
have grasped what this concept tries to think, calling it space or
matter is merely a question of names) is that not only intelligible
and sensible, but also intelligibility and intellection, sensibility
and sensation are one thing only. *Chora*-matter is the letting
itself be seen and known, the self-opening of the all and of each
thing: the unity of mind and matter in a perceptible god.

78 David di Dinant, *Mente Materia Dio* / Mens Hyle Deus (Emanuele Dattilo
ed.) (Genoa: Il nuovo melangolo, 2022). [The text is printed in original and
translation in Tristan Dagron, 'David of Dinant—On the Quaternuli Fragment
<Hyle, Mens, Deus>', *Revue de métaphysique et de morale* 4(40) (2003):
419–36; available online: http://rb.gy/6sgx86 (last accessed 1 October
2024). —Trans.]

Cognition is co-nascence, the joint birth of the knowable and the known in an auto-affection. To separate them as cause and effect, object and subject is the erring to which—having abandoned the thinking of *chora*—modernity has committed itself, grounding its science in this separation.

11. A mosaic in the narthex of the Church of the Chora in Istanbul represents,[79] betwixt two adoring angels, the Virgin with a child in her lap. An inscription on both sides of the female figure reads: *He chora tou achoretou*. The translation is not uncontentious, given that a literal version of the kind 'territory of the non-territorial' or even 'place of the unplaceable' seems unsatisfactory. As we're dealing with an image, which we moderns are accustomed to assigning to the domain of the visual arts, a translation such as 'figure of the non-figurable' or 'manifestation of the non-manifestable' may appear more adequate. But we only understand the meaning of this enigmatic syntagm if we see in it an extreme theological *Nachleben*, an afterlife of the Platonic *chora*, transferred from the sphere of philosophy into that of liturgy and the cult of images. Two scholars of byzantine art, Nicoletta Isar and Sotiria Kordi, have incisively limned this nexus. As Isar writes:

---

79 Formerly Church of St Saviour in Chora, now Kariye Mosque. [Trans.]

In the history of the Platonic *chôra*, there is an interesting case of appropriation of the term, which has not been enough discussed from the perspective of the Platonic dialogue itself. This is the Byzantine *chôra*—a most fascinating synthesis of Christian theology and anthropology, on the one hand, and Platonic metaphysics and mysticism, on the other.[80]

Kordi, analyzing the architectonic structure and the decorations of the church's *parekklesion*, suggests that

the space of the *parekklesion* can be seen in the light of the concept of the *chora*, as having the characteristics of a matrix, a space body in between and always in the making, in the process of becoming meaningful. By extension, one can imagine the *Chora parekklesion* as a *chora* space in Platonic terms.[81]

The connection with Platonic thought is, truth be told, even tighter, and concerns the conception of the status of images in the theological-political disputes that for more than a century pitted iconoclasts against iconophiles. At the centre of the implacable conflicts at the councils of Hieria, Nicea and Constantinople, we find the dogma of

---

80 Nicoletta Isar, '*Chôra*: Tracing the Presence', *Review of European Studies* 1(1) (2009): 42.

81 Sotiria Kordi, 'The Chora Parekklesion as a Space of Becoming' (PhD diss., University of Leeds, 2014), p. 277.

the Incarnation and that of the two natures (human and divine) of Christ. In Platonic terms, the problem is: how can a sensible image (the sensible is defined in the *Timaeus* as *eikon*) manifest the non-sensible (divine nature)? Or: how is it possible to experience in one and the same place the sensible and the non-sensible?

It is significant that In the theological disputes, concepts belonging to the technical vocabulary of painting are transformed into theological categories. In the *Statesman* (277c), anticipating the opposition between drawing and painting familiar to Renaissance and modern theorists, Plato had evoked the difference between the line that traces the contours of a figure (*perigraphe*, literally 'circumscription') and the colours that accord it vibrancy ('our discourse like a painted animal has its *perigraphe* adequately traced from outside but lacks the vibrancy [*nergeia*] that is obtained with dyes and the admixture of colours'). This concept is taken up again by the iconoclasts to affirm the non-figurability of divine nature. As Constantin V argued, because in Christ human nature and divine nature are indivisibly united in a single person (*prosopon*, which also means 'face' and 'mask'), it is not possible to depict him, for in so doing one would be circumscribing that which is uncircumscribable ('it is clear that he who has painted that *prosopon* has circumscribed the divine nature, which in itself is uncircumscribable'). Against this drastic simplification, Nikephorus objects by distinguishing, as Plato had done, between drawing (*perigraphe*), which makes something present, and painting (*graphe*), which does not possess this power:

> In the drawing it is necessarily present, in painting it is absolutely not present [...] a man in fact is painted [*graphetai*] in his own image but is not circumscribed [*ou perigraphetai*, is not drawn] within it, if not in the proper place of the circumscription. These two modes are indeed very distant, because a man is painted through colours and mosaics, if that is requested, shaping him in many colours and forms and with varying splendour. But in no way will it be possible to circumscribe him through these, for as we have said circumscribing is something else. Painting-inscription [*graphe*] makes present the corporeal form of the inscribed, imprinting its figure [*schema*], its form [*morphen*] and its likeness. Circumscription, instead, not having anything in common with these three elements, delimits the contour.[82]

The distinction between the two essential elements of pictorial practice (drawing and colour, or circumscription and inscription) is used here to legitimate the cult of images. Just as in the Platonic *chora* the intelligible makes

82 Nikephoros, *Antirrhetikos* in Jacques Paul Migne (ed.), *Patrologia Graeca*, VOL. 100 (Paris: Imprimerie Catholique, 1865), p. 357.

itself present by imprinting itself in an image, and just as, in the *Republic*'s simile, the sun—which is otherwise blinding—can be contemplated 'in its *chora*' (*en tei autou chorai*), so in painting the divine *achoretos* is present without being circumscribed (drawn) within it. In an analogous manner, the Madonna can be defined *chora* of Christ and the name of the Church (*Ecclesia tou agiou soteros en tei chorai*) can literally mean: the Saviour visible and present in his *chora*.

It is not surprising that the most ancient testimony of this syntagm (in the form *chora tou theou achoretou*, which appears at the beginning of *ikos* 8) is to be found in the Acathist Hymn to the mother of the Lord (*akathistos*, not sitting, meaning it was sung standing) in the byzantine liturgy. The liturgy is an ensemble of gestural figures and doxologies in which the divine becomes present: it is, in brief, a *choreography*.

CHAPTER THREE

Steresis

That Aristotle's assertion according to which 'Plato says in the *Timaeus* that matter and *chora* are the same thing' is tendentious is beyond doubt. Read carefully the passage in question:

> Hence Plato, too, says in the *Timaeus* that matter and *chora* are the same thing. For 'the participative' [*to metaleptikon*] and *chora* are one and the same thing. Though he made a different use of 'the participative' in what are called his 'unwritten doctrines' from that in the *Timaeus*, he still declared that place [*topos*] and *chora* were the same thing. While everyone says that place is something, he alone tried to say what it is.[1]

---

1 Aristotle, *Physics: Books III and IV*, p. 23 (209b11–16) [translation modified].

First, we need to explain the 'hence' (*diò*). In the immediately preceding lines, Aristotle speaks in fact of a possible, albeit for him unwarranted, identification between *topos* and matter:

> But [if one considers it] in the way in which *topos* is thought to be the extension of the magnitude, [*topos* is] the matter. For this [extension of the magnitude] is different from the magnitude; this is that which is surrounded and bounded by the *eidos*, as by a surface and a limit; and it is this kind of thing that matter and the indefinite are. For when the limit and the properties of the sphere are removed, nothing is left but the matter.[2]

Plato would have thus incurred the error of equating *topos* and *hyle*, place and matter. To level such an accusation at him, Aristotle must attribute to Plato an assertion that is nowhere to be found in the *Timaeus*, writing 'Hence Plato, too', etc. The following passage would somehow furnish proof of this false attribution: 'For "the participative" and *chora* are one and the same thing.' This assertion too is inexact: in the places where Plato defines *chora*, the term *metaleptikon*, which Aristotle seems to employ as a Platonic technical term, does not appear. Plato only writes (51b1) that 'the mother and matrix [. . .] is an invisible and amorphous *eidos*, all-receiving and which participates

2 Aristotle, *Physics: Books III and IV*, pp. 23–24 [translation modified].

[*metalambanon*] in a very aporetic and difficult way in the intelligible.' As we have seen, scholars have also shown that in the final dialogues the vocabulary of participation tends to be replaced by that of the paradigm. At this point, Aristotle attributes to Plato a further identification—of *chora* with the place—which is also absent from the *Timaeus*. The reference to the unwritten teachings, where one would find a different definition of *chora*, is reprised shortly thereafter; here the suggestion is that the participant was identified by Plato both with the large and the small as well as, 'as he wrote [*gegraphen*, almost as if to qualify the foregoing *phesin*, 'says'—G. A.] in the *Timaeus*, with matter' (209b33–210a1).

The Identity *chora-topos-hyle* is never proven but, so to speak, is always presupposed. Plato erred twice over, once because he identified *chora* with matter and a second time because he identified it with the place; but in fact, in a perfectly circular manner, it's the second mistake that precedes and produces the first. One begins by effectively suggesting that Plato identified the place with matter, and to prove it one attributes to Plato two assertions that he never uttered (that *chora* and *hyle* are the same thing and that *topos* and *chora* may be identified with one another). At this point, it's possible to conclude, thereby tempering the diagnosis of his twofold error, that Plato is still the only one who tried to define the place.

The circularity and tendentiousness of the argument are so evident that the task of the interpreter cannot be restricted to noting their falsity but requires trying to understand the reasons that could have induced the disciple to attribute to his teacher a thesis which he knew had not as such been professed by him. In any case, it is certainly not from this passage that we can learn what was really at stake in the transformation of the Platonic doctrine of *chora* into the Aristotelian doctrine of matter.

2. It is at the end of Book I of the *Physics* that Aristotle lays out his critique of the Platonic doctrine of matter while also detailing the difference that separates it from his own thinking. After having asserted that the most ancient philosophers (*oi proteron*, those who came first, namely, Parmenides and his school) had kept their distance 'from the path to coming to be, passing away, and change generally,'[3] thereby neglecting nature itself, Aristotle writes that others—that is to say, Platonists—had tried to know it, but in an inadequate way. They recognized that something is generated from non-being (*ek me ontos*) but they held that matter is one according to both number and power (*dynamis*). What Aristotle means is immediately specified: the difference between our thinking and theirs is that

---

3 Aristotle, *Physics: Books I and II* (William Charlton trans. and ed.) (Oxford: Clarendon Books, 1992), p. 20 (191b32).

> We for our part say that matter and privation [*steresis*] are different, and that the one, the matter, by virtue of concurrence is not-entity [*ouk on*], but is near to substance [*ousia*] and a substance in a way, whilst the other, the lack, in itself [*kath'auten*] is not-entity, and is not a substance at all. According to them, on the other hand, the great and the small, whether together or separate, are what is not-being [*me on*] in the same way.[4]

The Aristotelian doctrine of matter and his critique of *chora* are comprehensible only if we keep in mind the fact that in this occasion Aristotle develops one of his fundamental concepts, that of *steresis*, or privative opposition, which he states a little later in the form of a theorem: 'privation is in some way a form [*he steresis eidos pos estin*]' (193b20). While in mere absence (*apousia*) we have the negation of something, 'in privation instead is generated a certain underlying nature with respect to which it is called privation' (*Metaphysics* 1004a15–16). Plato's error is not to have recognized that matter is twofold, to the extent that it also contains within itself—both inseparable and distinct—privation. As Aristotle argues:

> They [the Platonists] got as far as seeing that there must be an underlying nature, but they made it one. And if someone calls it a pair, viz. great and

---

4 Aristotle, *Physics: Books I and II*, pp. 20–21 (192a1–9) [translation modified].

small, he is still doing the same thing, for he over-looked the other nature [i.e. privation]. The one remains, joint cause with the form of the things which come to be, as it were a mother. The other half of the opposition [that is, privation] you might often imagine, if you focus on its evil tendency, to be totally non-existent.[5]

As the citation of the Platonic metaphor of *chora* as mother underscores, Plato understood the importance of matter in generation but did not notice that privation constitutively belongs to it.

It is worth dwelling on the strategic importance of privative opposition, which will enjoy a long heritage in modern thought (in particular, the Hegelian dialectic would be unthinkable without it). Aristotle's discovery is in fact that something can be present in its lack, or, as he writes, that *steresis* is in some way an *eidos*, which conserves the form of that of which it is the privation. It is not by chance if in the philosophical vocabulary contained in Book Delta of the *Metaphysics* the definition of *steresis* follows that of 'having': the lack of that which one should have is something like a degree zero of having. In the *Physics*, however, Aristotle employs it to articulate his doctrine of genesis. 'everything comes to be out of the underlying matter and the form [*gignetai pan ek te tou hypokeimenou kai tes*

---

5 Aristotle, *Physics: Books I and II*, p. 21 (192a10–15).

morphes]';[6] but matter is one according to number, though double inasmuch as it implies privation: 'By that which is opposed, I mean the ignorant of music, by that which underlies, the man; and shapelessness, formlessness, disarray are opposed, and the bronze, the stone, the gold underlie'.[7] That is why for Aristotle the principles of genesis are not two but three (191a1): form, privation and matter. And because of this essential function that he ascribes to privation, he can write that the way in which Platonists conceive of the originary triad (intelligible, sensible, *chora*) is completely different from his (192a9).

The difference is indeed even more meaningful insofar as it concerns how one understands the ontological status of opposites. What is at stake in Plato is the knowability of two principles which, in their separation, lead to irreparable aporias: by offering them a space, *chora* somehow makes the sensible thinkable and the intelligible visible. And while *chora*, albeit devoid of its own form, does not in any way harbour an opposition and a privation, in the essential Aristotelian triad it is instead the dialectic between form and its opposite, *steresis*, for which matter simply serves as the passive substrate for generation. And while the Platonic dialectic tends towards the elimination of presuppositions to attain an anhypothetical *arké*, it is precisely on the presupposition of a *hypokeimenon*, of an under-lying in which

---

6 Aristotle, *Physics: Books I and II*, p. 17 (190b20) [translation modified].

7 Aristotle, *Physics: Books I and II*, p. 17 (191b16).

inheres a *steresis*—a privation understood in some way as a form—that the Aristotelian dialectic grounds its power.

If we wanted to define by a single trait the essential difference between the two conceptions, we could encapsulate it in the permanence or otherwise of a presupposition as dialectical foundation. In other words, we could say that both Plato and his disciple Aristotle proceed in the awareness of a presupposition, which is the effect of the specific power of *logos*, which pre-supposes that whereof one speaks (as Aristotle writes, 'all things are said in the presupposition of an under-lying [*cath'ypokeimenou*]', *Categories* 2a19). But while for Plato, as explicitly follows from *Republic* 511b, it's a question of eliminating this presupposition, by treating 'presuppositions not as principles, but as presuppositions, namely, as steps or moves towards the non-presupposed [*anypotheton*]', for Aristotle, on the contrary, the presupposed must be held on to, as happens in the *Physics* with matter and in the logic with the presupposition of the primary substance ('this man', 'Socrates'). On the one hand, it's a matter of coming to terms with the presupposing power of language, on the other, of grounding upon it, at least to a certain extent, the force of apophantic *logos*, which says something about something. And this is why Aristotle cannot but transform *chora*, which expresses the opening and knowability of entities, into *hyle* as 'the primary underlying', which nevertheless contains within it a privation that acts as a powerful dialectical principle of genesis and movement.

Aristotle's commentators, from Simplicius to Alexander of Aphrodisias, perfectly understood this trait of Aristotelian *hyle* and thematized it through the concept of *epitedeiotes*, of a disposition or aptitude of matter to receive forms. According to Alexander, 'the proper nature of matter consists in having a disposition [*ten epitedeiota echein*] by virtue of which it is capable of receiving quality', and this aptitude is 'intermediate between that thing and its privation [*metaxy ekeinou te kai tes stereseos autou*]'.[8] Matter is here the measure of an entity's capacity to be affected; it is no surprise that Alexander, reprising the Aristotelian image of the writing tablet, likens power not to the tablet but to the layer of sensitive wax that covers it. In his comment to Aristotle's *Physics*, Simplicius remarks about privation that it comes before form but also alongside and after it (*pro tou eidos kai meta to eidos*), inasmuch as it is 'an absence of the form, though with a suitability for it [*apousia tis meta epitedeiotetos tes pros to eidos*]'.[9] That is why, he adds, Aristotle rightly criticized Plato who, whilst affirming that in matter opposites—the large and the small—are present, did not notice that it contains a privation that manifests itself precisely as the 'receptivity of opposites [*pros ta antikeimena epitedeioteta*]'.[10]

---

8 Alexander of Aphrodisias, *Quaestiones 1.1–2.15* (R. W. Sharples trans.), Ancient Commentators on Aristotle (Richard Sorabji series ed.) (London: Bloomsbury, 2014), p. 103 (QUES. 2.7).

9 Simplicius, *On Aristotle Physics 1.5–9*, p. 92 (212.7–8).

10 Simplicius, *On Aristotle Physics 1.5–9*, p. 104 (222.31).

That in the Aristotelian critique of the Platonic doctrine of matter privation plays an essential function is something that Calcidius understands perfectly well, as evinced by his paraphrase of Aristotle's text.

> For here is what [Aristotle] says: 'To us, then, matter [*silva*] will appear to be distinct from privation [*carentia*, the term underlines the particular meaning of *steresis*, G. A.], in the sense that matter is something existent only incidentally whereas privation is nothing in the primary and absolute sense; and whereas matter has something approaching substance, there is no substance whatsoever of privation. And others,' he says, 'who take the wrong view think that privation and matter are one thing, for they call the same thing small and big and reduce two things that should be viewed separately to one and the same thing and suppose that a single determinate thing acts as a substrate for bodies. And although they divide it into the greater and smaller, so as to make two, one thing is indicated and another omitted despite the duality; for matter, like a mother, cooperates in the formation of bodies, whereas privation does not cooperate in the formation but rather impedes and resists to the extent that, while form is a divine and desirable thing, privation is contrary to it; but matter seeks form and clarity and by its very nature is desirous of it. Moreover, if privation were to seek form then it must seek its own contrary, and yet all contrariety occasions destruction; privation, then, will not desire its own destruction.' [. . .] Aristotle makes these points in support of his views on the first principles of reality and the nature of matter; but his language, being rather

obscure, seems in need of explanation. He poses three origins for the universe [*tres origines universae rei*]: form, matter, and privation [*species, silva, carentia*].[11]

3. We have insisted up to now on the most obvious traits that differentiate the Aristotelian theory of matter from the Platonic theory of *chora*. Yet these must present some analogies and likenesses, without which such a stubborn and enduring identification of *chora* with *hyle* would not have been possible. Both ancient commentators and modern exegetes have observed that in both we are dealing with a being-in. We have already signalled the convergence of *chora* and matter in the *en hoi*, the 'where.' However, the identification of matter with the place in which each body finds itself is just what Aristotle wants to distance himself from. Even when the time comes to define his theory of the place, he evokes, taking his cue from a citation of Hesiod on the originary chaos, the mistaken idea according to which 'it was necessary that there should first be a space [*chora*] available to the things that are, because he thinks as most people do that everything is somewhere and in place.'[12]

11 Calcidius, *On Plato's 'Timaeus'*, pp. 573–77.

12 Aristotle, *Physics: Books III and IV*, p. 21 (208b31–32).

If an analogy exists it must instead be looked for—
this is the hypothesis that we intend to advance—in the
noetic rather than the ontological aspect of the two doctrines. In the exposition of the *Timaeus* there is in effect a
point where there appears something like a *steresis*, a privation that nevertheless conserves something of that which
it is lacking. I am referring to the passage (52b2) which we
have already tarried with, in which Plato describes the
modality of knowledge of the third kind, which 'can be
touched in a reasoning of the bastard kind [*logismoi tini
nothoi*] with an absence of sensation [*met'anaisthesias*]'.
We have seen how the singular expression *meth'anaisthesias*
does not simply mean 'without sensation', but implies, so
to speak, the perception of an anaesthesia, the transformation of a lack of sensation into something positive, namely,
into the possession of a power or capacity to feel that is
not actually exercised. The Aristotelian doctrine of matter
is a doctrine of power; an essential part of this doctrine—
as the philosopher does not tire of repeating against those
who hold that power exists only in the act of its exercise—
is that it exists properly and above all as powerlessness or
impotence (*adynamia*), that is to say as the capacity not to
pass to the act (*dynamis me energein*). As he writes in the
Metaphysics: 'Powerlessness is merely the lack or privation
[*steresis*] of the corresponding power [*dynamis*]. Every
power is powerlessness of the same and with regard to the
same [*tou autou kai kata to auto pasa dynamis adynamia*].'[13]

---

13 Aristotle, *Metaphysics*, p. 182 (1046a29–32) [translation modified].

In this sense, power is above all the possession of a *steresis*, the having of a lack: 'sometimes', we read in the *Metaphysics* 'being powerful seems to imply possessing something, and sometimes it means to be deprived of something. But if privation is in itself a *hexis*, a habit, the powerful is such, either because it has a certain *hexis* or because it has its privation.'[14] Before every passage to the act, power affects itself; it is, so to speak, *potentia potentiae*, power of power.

The hypothesis we are proposing is that the Aristotelian conception of *adynamia* is really a development of the *anaisthesia* that in the *Timaeus* makes possible the perception of the *chora*. Just as the space of the *chora* opens up only at the point in which we perceive our own anaesthesia, so matter and power are given above all in the form of an *adynamia*, of a capacity not to pass to the act, of a pure and formless lying-under every form and every act, and first of all lying-under themselves:

> Matter according to power [*kata dynamin*] does not in itself pass away, but can neither be brought to be nor destroyed [. . .] If it were generated, there would have to be something underlying [*hypokestai ti*], out of which and in which it came to be; that, however, is its nature, to be before it is generated (I call matter that which primarily underlies [*to proton hypocheimenon*] every thing).[15]

14 Aristotle, *Metaphysics*, p. 105 (1019b5–8) [translation modified].

15 Aristotle, *Physics: Books I and II*, p. 21 (192a26–31) [translation modified].

In terms of Aristotelian categories, *chora* and matter—
otherwise remote from one another—communicate
through their constitutive nexus with power: in the
met'anaisthesias of the *Timaeus* as the givenness of a capacity to feel without an object, in *adynamia* as the possession
of a privation, the capacity not to pass to the act. As is his
wont, Aristotle, always quick to detail what distinguishes
his thinking from that of his master, prefers not to thematize
the motifs which he has received or reprised from Plato.

CHAPTER FOUR

Sensorium Dei

1. We encounter a remarkable resurgence of the Platonic doctrine of *chora* in the thinking of one of the foremost founders of modern science, Isaac Newton. If science always harbours an element of poetic imagination, the Newtonian thesis of space as *sensorium Dei* is one of the highest poetic moments in the history of Western science. The thesis, formulated, with some variations, in the *Queries* of the *Opticks*, beginning with the Latin edition of 1706, elicited both enthusiasm and diffidence among his contemporaries. In *Query* 23 of that edition, it reads: *Annon spatium universum, sensorium est Entis Incorporei, Viventis et Intelligentis; quod res ipsas cernat et complectatur intimas, totasque penitus et in se praesentes perspiciat; quarum id quidem, quod in nobis sentit et cogitate, Imagines tantum in cerebro contuetur.*[1]

---

1 In *Query* 28 of the 1717 English edition of the *Opticks*, the argument is rendered as follows: 'does it not appear from Phaenomena that there is a Being incorporeal, living, intelligent, omnipresent, who in infinite Space, as

Though, when the book's first copies had already been printed, the identity between space and *sensorium* was tempered by the introduction of a *tamquam*, 'as it were' (*esse Entem Incorporeum, Viventem, Intelligentem, Omnipraesentem, qui in spatio infinito* tamquam *in sensorio suo res ipsas intime cernat*), the thesis already elicited in his contemporaries—save for some enthusiastic accord, like that of Joseph Addison, who judged it 'the noblest and most exalted Way of considering this infinite Space'—diffidence and disquiet. Yet we are not dealing, as it has been repeatedly claimed, with a necessarily imprecise metaphor, but with a philosophical notion whose genealogy we can trace and of which we can offer a passably clear definition.

A reading of *De gravitatione et aequipondio fluidorum et solidorum in fluidis* (On the gravity and equal weight of fluid and solid bodies in fluids), a posthumous work by Newton dated by his editors to the end of the 1660s, shows that the necessary connection between God and space is elaborated in the context of a radical questioning of the Cartesian identification of the body and extension. As Newton writes:

---

it were in his Sensory, sees the things themselves intimately, and throughly [*sic*] perceives them, and comprehends them wholly by their immediate presence to himself: Of which things the Images only carried through the Organs of Sense into our little Sensoriums, are there seen and beheld by that which in us perceives and thinks.' Isaac Newton, *Opticks, or, A Treatise of the Reflections, Refractions, Inflections & Colours of Light* (New York: Dover, 1952), p. 370. [Trans.]

Descartes [...] seems to have demonstrated that
body does not differ at all from extension, abstracting hardness, colour, weight, cold, heat, and the
remaining qualities which body can lack, so that
at last there remains only its extension in length,
width, and depth, which therefore alone pertain
to its essence.[2]

To refute this argument means for Newton to unsettle 'the
principal foundation of Cartesian philosophy' and implies
the preliminary definition of 'what extension and body
are, and how they differ from each other.'[3] And it is here
that Newton advances some ontological theses that we
must attentively examine. We might expect, he writes, that
extension is defined as substance or as accident or as
nothing, but 'by no means, for it has its own manner of
existing which is proper to it [*proprium existendi modum*].'[4]
What is particularly significant is the reason that leads one
to exclude that it is substance: 'It is not substance: on the
one hand, because it is not absolute in itself, but is as it
were an emanative effect of God and an affection of every
kind of being [*tamquam Deo effectus emanativus, et omnis
entis affectio quaedam*].'[5] What is the provenance of the

---

2 Isaac Newton, *Philosophical Writings* (Andrew Janiak ed.) (Cambridge:
Cambridge University Press, 2004), p. 21.

3 Newton, *Philosophical Writings*, p. 21.

4 Newton, *Philosophical Writings*, p. 21.

5 Newton, *Philosophical Writings*, p. 21.

singular expression *Dei effectus emanativus* and what does it mean? It is well known that Newton was influenced by the thought of Henry More but in this case the derivation is undeniable and specific. Axiom 16 of one of More's most widely read books, *The Immortality of the Soul*, which Newton had annotated as a student at Cambridge, declares: 'By an Emanative Cause is understood such a Cause as merely by Being, no other activity or causality interposed, produces an Effect.'[6] The next axiom therefore concludes: 'An Emanative Effect is coexistent with the very Substance of that of which is said to be the Cause thereof.'[7]

Let us reflect on the special ontological modality that defines extension as an emanative effect; divine substance, by the sole fact of existing, makes an extension be, but this extension is not distinct from it as an object created at a certain moment, but instead coexists eternally with it. The concept of *affectio*, which Newton introduces immediately afterwards, defines this special ontological modality of extension: it is not an attribute or quality that is added to substance from the outside, according to the model of a substantialist ontology of the Aristotelian type; rather, in keeping with the paradigm of a modal ontology, it is an affection or mode of being that always already follows immediately from its existence.

---

6 Henry More, *The Immortality of the Soul* (A. Jacob ed.) (Dordrecht: Martinus Nijhoff, 1987[1662]), p. 37.

7 More, *Immortality of the Soul*, p. 38.

From this perspective, the correspondence between Samuel Clarke and G. W. Leibniz offers some instructive insights. Responding to Leibniz, who objects to Newton that if one affirms that space is a real and absolute being it will then need to be eternal and infinite ('Hence some [the cabalists] have believed [space] to be God himself, or one of his attributes, his immensity. But since space consists of parts, it is not a thing that can belong to God'),[8] Clarke, speaking for his mentor Newton, argues that space is not a being or a thing, but rather 'a property or a consequence' that depends on the existence of an infinite and eternal being and, as such, is not other than or outside of God.[9] Yet Newton must not have been satisfied with the definition of space as a 'property', for, writing to the editor of the correspondence, he asked him to specify in the introduction that if, 'through an inevitable imperfection of language,' he employed the terms property or quality, this was not, however, in the sense in which these terms are used by those who deal with logic or metaphysics; rather, 'by this name he means only that space and duration are modes of existence of the Substance which is really necessary, and substantially omnipresent and eternal.'[10] The reference to

---

8 Gottfried Wilhelm Leibniz and Samuel Clarke, *Correspondence* (Roger Ariew ed.) (Indianapolis, IN, and Cambridge: Hackett, 2020), p. 14.

9 Leibniz and Clarke, *Correspondence*, p. 19.

10 Quoted in *The Leibniz–Clarke Correspondence* (H. G. Alexander ed.) (Manchester: Manchester University Press, 1956), p. *xxix*.

a modal ontology of a Spinozist type is evident: extension is not a property or an attribute of the divine substance, but one of the modes in which it exists, one of its affections or modifications.

In Spinoza's *Ethics*, the relation between God and the finite modes is expressed by being affected ('By mode I understand the affections of a substance[11] [*per modum intelligo substantiae affectiones*]'):

> what is finite and has a determinate existence could not have been produced by the absolute nature of an attribute of God [. . .] It had, therefore, to follow either from God or from an attribute of God insofar as it is considered to be affected by some mode [*debuit ergo ex Deo, vel aliquo eius attributo sequi, quatenus aliquo modo affectum consideratur*]).[12]

Affection or the capacity to be affected is one of the fundamental concepts of the *Ethics*, but its comprehension should not be taken for granted.

2. It is significant that, by insisting on the concept of *affectio* (which radicalizes the Aristotelian doctrine of the *pathe tou ontos*, the 'passions' that touch on being as such) to

---

11 Spinoza, *Ethics*, PART 1, DEF. 5, p. 85.

12 Spinoza, *Ethics*, PART 1, PROP. 28, p. 103.

define the nature of space, Newton quotes the passage from the *Timaeus* on *chora*, in which Plato says that what exists must be in a place and that what is neither on earth nor in the heavens is not nothing:

> Space is an affection of a being just as a being [*entis quatenus ens affectio*]. No being exists or can exist which is not related to space in some way. God is everywhere, created minds are somewhere [*alicubi*], and body is in the space that it occupies; and whatever is neither everywhere nor anywhere does not exist. And hence it follows that space is an emanative effect of the first existing being, for if any being whatsoever is posited, space is posited.[13]

Newton notes that this does not mean that space is the body of God and that no one 'should for this reason imagine God to be like a body, extended [*ad instar corporis extendi*] and made of divisible parts.'[14] What is at stake in space is rather God's mode of its presence in the world, for 'any being has a manner proper to itself of being present in spaces.'[15] Space is the very presence of God in the world:

> If ever space had not existed, God at that time would have been nowhere [*nullibi adfuerit*]; and hence he either created space later (where he was

---

13 Newton, *Philosophical Writings*, p. 25.

14 Newton, *Philosophical Writings*, p. 26.

15 Newton, *Philosophical Writings*, p. 26.

not present himself), or else, which is no less
repugnant to reason, he created his own ubiquity.
Next, although we can possibly imagine that there
is nothing in space, yet we cannot think that space
does not exist [*tamen non possumus cogitare non
esse spatium*].

Yet again, this last argument, which will have a lasting
influence, is drawn from More. In his *Antidote Against
Atheism*, having affirmed that if there were no matter, the
immensity of the divine essence would occupy with its
ubiquity all of space—which would be nothing but, as it
were, '*the Replication*, as I may so speak, of his indivisible
substance'—More adds that space is something 'which we
cannot disimagine in our Phancy' and that this 'unavoidable imagination of the necessity of *an Infinite Space*' is
proof of God's necessary existence.[16]

If we cannot imagine that space is not, this is because
it is not an autonomous substance but only an affection or
emanative effect (More will also speak of an *Amplitude*
and an *Immensity*) of divine substance, the very mode of
its presence to the world. But, Newton will add, the existence of space does not depend on the existence of the
world because, 'space is no more space where the world

---

16 Henry More, 'An Appendix to the Foregoing Antidote against Atheism' in
A Collection of Several Philosophical Writings (London: J. Flesher, 1662),
p. 163.

exists, than where there is no world, unless perchance you would say that when God created the world in this space he at the same time created space in itself.'[17]

3. It is at this point that the analogies with the Platonic doctrine of *chora* make themselves forcefully present. For More, who represents the tradition of Oxford and Cambridge Platonism, from which Newton seems to draw his philosophical conceptuality, the object of metaphysics is not, as in scholastic tradition, being as being (*ens quatenus ens*), which he ascribes to the competency of logic (*Ens quatenus ens non est Obiectum Metaphysicae, sed Logicae*),[18] but something that lies, so to speak, beyond (or on the hither side of) being. This something is incorporeal substance, whose first example is, indeed, 'the existence of an immovable extension distinct from matter, which is commonly called Space or inner Place.'[19] This space, 'is not an imaginary entity [*Imaginarium quiddam*] but is real, or rather Divine.'[20] In what concerns us, 'whether we think it or do not think it [*sive de ea cogitemus sive non cogitemus*] we cannot not think [*non possumus non concipere*] that there has always existed and will eternally exist a certain

---

17 Newton, *Philosophical Writings*, p. 27.

18 Henry More, *Enchiridion Metaphysicum sive de rebus incorporis, per H. More Cantabrigiensem* (London: E. Flesher, 1671), p. 5.

19 More, *Enchiridion Metaphysicum*, p. 42.

20 More, *Enchiridion Metaphysicum*, p. 64.

immovable Extension that infinitely pervades all things, and is really distinct from movable matter.'[21]

What is significant here, exactly as in the *Timaeus*, is the modality in which we know this infinite extension: we cannot not think it, or better, we cannot not imagine it. The reality of space is not something that we know through a free exercise of the faculty of thought or imagination; it is, rather, something that we cannot 'disimagine.' What status of the imagination (and, in general, of cognition) corresponds to a powerlessness not to imagine [*non potere non immaginare*]? Here imagination and thought—as in the bastard kind of reasoning of the *chora*, perceived 'with an anaesthesia'—do not perceive an external object, but their own powerlessness to cease imagining, before or in the absence of bodies or beings to perceive. The imagination that cannot disimagine, imagines space, imagines a pure opening, 'an infinite extension that surrounds on every side a finite matter.'[22] And this, like *chora*, is not a thing, but a pure emanative effect of existence, the pure givenness of the world as a perceptible God which, as the Pythagoreans suggest, 'is said to breathe in this space [*respirare dicatur in hoc Spatio*].'[23] To a space that is a pure auto-affection of substance there corresponds a 'powerlessness to disimagine' that is a pure auto-affection of the imagination.

---

21 More, *Enchiridion Metaphysicum*, p. 6.

22 More, *Enchiridion Metaphysicum*, p. 43.

23 More, *Enchiridion Metaphysicum*, p. 66.

Through the concept of *dynamis*, Aristotle contributed to transforming into the faculties of a subject what were really its affections. Even if in Aristotle there cannot strictly speaking be a theory of the subject, it is significant that he invoked the concept of will, alien to classical thought, specifically with regard to power's passage to the act (thought passes to the act 'when it wills it [*hopotan bouletai*]', *De anima*, 417b24); in this way, a capacity to be affected becomes a faculty that the subject can dispose of. The capacity to be affected is something different from the act of a knowing subject, and if we conceived intellection and sensibility above all as affections of a being and not as faculties or powers, the whole theory of knowledge would need to be rethought from scratch.

4. It is only starting from this rigorous ontological categorization that we can understand the doctrine of space as *sensorium Dei* that appears in the *Opticks*. Once again, the correspondence between Clarke and Leibniz furnishes some important details. To Leibniz, who criticizes Newton because the latter asserts 'that space is an organ which God makes use of to perceive things by', Clarke replies that the *sensorium* is not an organ for Newton, but the very presence of God to things and in things, through which he perceives and knows the world.[24] And when Leibniz objects in turn that the 'reason why God consciously perceives everything is not his bare presence, but also his operation,' and that

---

24 Leibniz and Clarke, *Correspondence*, pp. 4–5.

he 'preserves things by an action that continually produces whatever is good and perfect in them,' and is obviously cognizant of what he is doing,[25] Clarke replies that God does not perceive things inasmuch as—according to the scholastic paradigm of continuous creation—he acts upon them, but simply 'by his being a living and intelligent, as well as an omnipresent substance.'[26] While Newton had deemed it prudent, to avoid the accusation of pantheism, to insert a *tamquam* (as it were) to mitigate the radicality of his thesis, the identity between space and God's *sensorium* is not a mere metaphor. God does not perceive things by means of space, as though the latter were an organ, but immediately *in* space, because the latter is the sensible form of his presence and, at the same time, his *sensorium*. In other words, space is not a reality external to God, but an affection of God's very sensibility as a living and thinking being.

The decisive problem which is at stake here is that of thinking the non-separation between God and the world, without falling back into their inert identity with one another. Extension conceived as an auto-affection or an emanative effect of the divine substance distinct from matter is what allows one to think this non-separation. God and the world are, so to speak, coextensive, and the space in which things and bodies are situated is the very

---

25 Leibniz and Clarke, *Correspondence*, p. 9.

26 Leibniz and Clarke, *Correspondence*, p. 12.

presence of God and, at the same time, the *sensorium* in which he perceives them. It is this immanence that Leibniz wants to exclude by reasserting the 'otherworldly' character of God. As he writes to Clarke, waving the pantheist scare-crow in his direction: 'I do not think I can be rightly blamed for saying that God is *intelligentia supramundana*! Will they say that he is *intelligentia mundana*, that is, the soul of the world? I hope not. However, they will do well to take care not to fall into that notion unawares.'[27]

The extreme intimacy and almost coincidence between God and space explains why both More and Newton felt close to the cabalistic doctrine according to which God's true name is Makom, the place, and why, on the other hand, Leibniz saw in this closeness the ambiguity that plagued the Newtonian doctrine. As More observed, that the conception of an immense originary space distinct from matter is really a representation of divine essence, 'accords wonderfully with the doctrine of the cabalists who, according to Cornelius Agrippa, list place among the attributes of God.'[28] Shortly before this passage, having itemized no less than twenty divine attributes or names, he adds in passing: 'not to mention how God among the cabalists is called Makom, or the Place [*ipsum Divinum Nomen apud Cabbalistas appellari Makom, id est locum*].'[29]

---

27 Leibniz and Clarke, *Correspondence*, p. 10.

28 More, *Enchiridion Metaphysicum*, p. 74.

The doctrine of light of Robert Grosseteste, master at Oxford in the thirteenth century, presents some analogies with More's doctrine of space. The unprecedented thesis that Grosseteste advances in his treatise *On Light* is that of the identity between light and the form of bodies: 'The first corporeal form which some call corporeity [*corporeitatem*] is in my opinion light.'[30] We need to distinguish here between what Grosseteste calls 'corporeity' (or the 'first form of bodies') and matter. In the narrative of *Genesis*, God in effect first created light, because it is light that—propagating by its nature in every direction within an infinite sphere—grants all bodies their form and their dimensions in space.

> [A] form that is in itself simple and without dimension could not introduce dimension in every direction into matter, which is likewise simple and without dimension, except by multiplying itself and diffusing itself instantaneously in every direction and thus extending matter in its own diffusion. For the form cannot desert matter, because it is inseparable from it and matter itself cannot be deprived of form.[31]

A true precursor of More's theses on space is Thomas Bradwardine, Doctor of Theology at Oxford in the first half of the 1300s. The corollary in five parts of Chapter 5 of Book 1 of his treatise *De causa Dei* imperatively declares:

---

29 More, *Enchiridion Metaphysicum*, p. 70.

30 Robert Grosseteste, *On Light* (Clare C. Riedl trans. and ed.) (Milwaukee: Marquette University Press, 1942), p. 10.

31 Grosseteste, *On Light*, p. 10.

242 · GIORGIO AGAMBEN

that God, essentially and presentially [*essentialiter et presentialiter*] is everywhere, not only in the world and all its parts, but also outside the world in the imaginary infinite place or void [*in situ seu vacuo imaginario infinito*]. That is why he can truly be called immense and uncircumscribed, though he is also said to be immense and uncircumscribed for other reasons [. . .] It is therefore evident that there can be a void of bodies but never and in no way a void of God. It manifestly follows that God is everywhere in the world.

This intimate presence or nigh-on 'infusion' of God in the world does not depend on creation but is coeternal with God:

God did not make the world like the artificer, outside of whom lies the arc he built, which, while it is being built, is in another place, so that, albeit in contact, the artificer resides in another place and is therefore extrinsic to what he builds. God instead fabricates while infused in the world [*Deus autem infuses mundo fabricat*] and fabricates while being everywhere and does not separate himself from the world in any way; he does not pour from outside the mass that he fabricates, he makes what he makes with the presence of his majesty and with his presence he governs what he makes. Thus he was in the world, and thus was the world made [. . .] God was in it eternally for himself and for the same reason he was everywhere in the void or in the imaginary infinite space and he is still everywhere outside the world.[32]

32 Thomas Bradwardine, *Thomae Bradwardini* [. . .] *De causa Dei contra Pelagium* [. . .] *libri tres* (London, 1618), pp. 177ff. See also Alexandre

5. The time has come to understand in all its implications what is at play in the obstinacy with which More and Newton affirm the difference between extension and matter (or body). For both, the polemical target is the commanding Cartesian thesis of the identity of matter and extension (in More's words, the *mutua materiae et extensio reciprocatio*) and the equally stringent Hobbesian theorem in Chapter 34 of the *Leviathan* according to which, because 'substance and body signify the same thing [...] substance incorporeal are words, which, then they are joined together, destroy one another.' That is why Newton and More, though affirming the reality of space, prefer to speak of an affection, an emanative effect or a mode of existence—and not of substance. But we still need to figure out what is meant by the syntagm 'immaterial extension'. It is not a question— as in a common mistake sometimes made by those who theorize it—of thinking space as a matter freed from its corporeity, like the emptiness left behind by a moving body. What the mind perceives when, in its special way, it thinks Platonic *chora* or Newtonian space, is not an object nor an essence nor simply the place in which that object finds itself; instead, it is the pure auto-affection of the being, its 'mode' of existing and presenting itself, its 'how'. If, as Newton does not tire of repeating, space is *entis quatenus ens affectio* (the affection of a being as being) and *posito*

Koyré, *Études d'histoire de la pensée philosophique* (Paris: Gallimard, 1971), pp. 82–84.

quolibet ente ponitur spatio (if any being whatsoever is posited, space is posited), what is the relation between a being and its spatial affection, its mode of existing and spacing? And, more generally, how are we to think the relation—if we can still speak of relation here—between a being and its affections or between a substance and its modes of being?

It is clear that the relation does not obtain here between two things or two separate terms, but between a thing and its appearing and making itself known, between a being and its knowability or appearance. To distinguish it from a substantial relation, we can call this relation between a being and its appearance 'phenomenological relation'. What is at stake here is not the relation between two beings in the world, between a knowing subject and a known object, but between a being and what we could call, according to the abovementioned etymology of the term *spatium* from *patere*, 'being open', its 'patency' or opening, which medieval thought still knew by the name *intentio*. And this opening is not in its turn a substance, but a pure mode— not a *quid* or a what, but only a 'how'.

Modern thought is born, in the very era that concerns us, with the repression of this relation, especially at the hands of Descartes. Identifying extension and matter, Descartes, as he explicitly declares on several occasions, jettisoned medieval philosophy's useless swarming of immaterial *intentiones*. But this really means that he put out of bounds the phenomenological relation between a being and its appearance, a thing and its knowability. Between bodies and thought, between *res extensa* and *cogitatio*, there is no need for any mediality. Knowledge is nothing but a relation between the knowing subject and the known object. If the Platonic tradition pondered the problem not of the knowledge of beings but of their knowability, namely, of the relation between a thing and what makes it knowable, now this relation is cast enduringly into the shadows. One will have to wait until Kant for it to present itself anew, even if in the truncated form of an unknowable thing in itself which limits the knowledge of appearances (*Erscheinungen*); but it is only with Heidegger that it will be thematized again—albeit with all the difficulties and contradictions implicit in accepting the framework of Aristotelian ontology—in the form of the difference between being and beings.

To repropose, as we have tried to do here, the problem of the *chora* and of space means recalling that between the intelligible and the sensible, and between knowledge and its object, there is a *tertium*, and that the task that still and always awaits thought is that of contemplating a being in its *chora* or, in Hölderlin's words, 'in the medium of its appearance', *in dem Mittel (moyen) seiner Erscheinung*[33]— in its 'how'.

---

33 Friedrich Hölderlin, *Anmerkung zum Oedipus* in *Hölderlin Sämtliche Werke*, VOL. 5 (F. Beissner ed.) (Stuttgart: Kohlhammer, 1954), p. 213.

Appendix

Lecture for the Competitive Examination for Associate Professor

The topic of this lecture is: Kant, Heidegger and the problem of aesthetics. So, I will not confine myself to a simple historical reconstruction of the relationship between these two authors but, taking my bearings from a fundamental aesthetic category—that of appearance—I will try to adumbrate the philosophical problem that I take to be at the centre of this relationship. The wager is thus to set out—to the degree possible and with the caveats required by a university lecture—a genuinely philosophical problem.

The central thesis of Heidegger's monograph on Kant—*Kant and the Problem of Metaphysics*, published in 1929, but written concurrently with *Being and Time*—is the assertion of the autonomy—and in a certain sense the priority—of the transcendental imagination as the 'fundamental source' of cognition next to the other two *Grundquellen*,

This is the text of a 1987 lecture for the competitive examination for associate professor of aesthetics. As will be evident, this lecture foreshadows some key themes in *The Unrealizable*.

sensibility and understanding.[1] To this end, and with the hermeneutic violence he has so often been chided for, Heidegger subjects to painstaking analysis a series of passages from the first edition of the *Critique of Pure Reason*, which Kant either suppressed or altered in the second edition. According to Heidegger, in the definitive edition Kant would have retreated in the face of that unknown root of every cognition that sprung up in the transcendental imagination. The latter thus ceased to be a faculty in its own right, losing its character as the fount of cognition to be demoted in relation to the understanding, which thereby gained the prerogative of serving as the origin of every synthesis. The three fundamental sources of cognition were thereby reduced to two: sensibility and the understanding, receptivity and spontaneity. The abyss that the transcendental imagination had opened for reason closed back up, not without leaving within the text the traces of its line of suture. As Heidegger writes: 'In the radicalism of his questions, Kant brought the "possibility" of metaphysics to this abyss. He saw the unknown. He had to shrink back.'[2]

I will instead seek to show that in truth Kant never stopped gazing into the abyss, and moreover that he tackled it again in the *Critique of Judgement* and that, finally, in the unfinished work of his final years, he confronted it in the most explicit and radical way.

1 Kant, *Critique of Pure Reason*, p. 193 (A50/B74).

2 Martin Heidegger, *Kant and the Problem of Metaphysics*, 5th EDN (Richard Taft trans.) (Bloomington, IN: Indiana University Press, 1997), p. 118.

I would like to begin my analysis with the concept of 'appearance', *Schein*. You will recall that, at the end of the 'Transcendental Analytic', shortly before stating the distinction of all objects into phenomena and noumena, Kant describes the 'land of truth' as an island enclosed within unsurpassable frontiers and surrounded by the ocean of appearance. 'This land,' he writes,

> is an island, and enclosed in unalterable bound-
> aries by nature itself. It is the land of truth (a
> charming name), surrounded by a broad and
> stormy ocean, the true seat of illusion, where many
> a fog bank and rapidly melting iceberg pretend to
> be new lands and, ceaselessly deceiving with empty
> hopes the wandering voyager looking around for
> new discoveries, entwine him in adventures from
> which he can never escape and yet also never bring
> to an end.[3]

A little further, concerning the distinction between phenomena and noumena, Kant once again invokes 'an illusion that is difficult to avoid [*eine schwer zu vermeidende Täuschung*]',[4] which pushes one illegitimately to extend the use of the categories of the understanding—which can refer only to the data of sensible intuitions—beyond the objects of experience.

---

3 Kant, *Critique of Pure Reason*, p. 339 (A236/B295) [translation modified].

4 Kant, *Critique of Pure Reason*, p. 359 (A248/B305) [translation modified].

This concept of 'appearance' and the correlated one of 'illusion' also recur in the subsequent remark 'On the amphiboly of concepts of reflection'. But it is in the Transcendental Dialectic, which Kant pointedly defines as a 'logic of appearance' (*Logik des Scheins*)[5] that the concept is developed to its extreme consequences, making its paradoxical character explicit. Here, in effect, appearance—which Kant calls transcendental—is no longer simply 'difficult to avoid' but properly 'unavoidable' (*unvermeidliche*). Kant here writes that transcendental appearance, unlike logical appearance, does not cease appearing even when its deception is recognized. While logical appearance dissolves as soon as it has been identified:

> Transcendental appearance [. . .] does not cease even though it is uncovered and its nullity is clearly seen into by transcendental criticism. [. . .] The transcendental dialectic will therefore content itself with uncovering the appearance in transcendental judgements, while at the same time protecting us from being deceived by it; but it can never bring it about that transcendental appearance [. . .] should even disappear and cease to be an appearance. For what we have to do with here is a natural and unavoidable illusion.[6]

5 Kant, *Critique of Pure Reason*, p. 384 (A293/B249) [translation modified].

6 Kant, *Critique of Pure Reason*, p. 386 (A298/B354) [translation modified]. [Where Guyer and Wood, following Kant's distinction between *Erscheinung*

While we are accustomed to thinking of appearance as something which, in fading, lets truth appear, we are confronted here with the paradox of a *Schein* that persists after its unveiling, in other words, an appearance that is properly speaking inextinguishable. From this point of view, the *Critique* presents itself as a journey that goes farther and farther into appearance, enfolding itself into ever more inextricable forms of *Schein*—and the philosopher as a 'wandering voyager' who experiences the insuppressible character of his own illusion. But what does this appearance consist of? How and why is it produced? And why, even when it is recognized as such, is it not extinguished?

Kant—this is one of the arguments in the Analytic and the Transcendental Dialectic to which he returns repeatedly—suggests that what happens here is that we confuse the transcendental use of the categories with their empirical use, and we thereby take the pure object of the understanding—the something in general = x—as a determinate object. In other words, we employ categories that have a purely transcendental meaning but no use (terms, as we might say today, which lack any denotation, any *Bedeutung*), as if they instead referred to an object of experience.

The understanding refers to an object that refers to nothing. The only legitimate way of thinking the noumenon

and *Schein*, render *Transzendentaler Schein* as 'transcendental illusion' and translate *Erscheinung* as 'appearance', Agamben here translates *Schein* as *apparenza*, 'appearance'. —Trans.]

is therefore to think of it as a *Grenzbegriff*, a limit-concept, in which nothing is thought save for the pure form of a concept in general. This limit concept too is unavoidable, but it gives us no object, except for an empty space. So why—let us again ask—is an appearance produced in this empty space; why does an unavoidable but empty concept produce an equally unavoidable appearance? Is there not in this void something that escapes us and of which appearance is the trace? Kant limits himself to reiterating that

> thinking precede[s] all possible determination of the arrangement of representations. We therefore think something in general, and on the one side determine it sensibly, only we also distinguish the object represented in general and *in abstracto* from this way of intuiting it; thus there remains to us a way of determining it merely through thinking that is, to be sure, a merely logical form without content, but that nevertheless seems to us [*scheint*] to be a way in which the object exists in itself (*noumenon*), without regard to the intuition to which our sensibility is limited.[7]

What Kant does not explain is how this 'logical form without content [*blosse logische Form ohne Inhalt*]' can *scheinen*, how it can appear and shine (one of the meanings of the German verb). Why does a kind of intentionality persist

---

7 Kant, *Critique of Pure Reason*, p. 381 (A289/B346).

here, a referring to something, when there is no object to which one can refer? How can there be in the understanding a receptivity that seems to precede the one contained in sensibility? If here nothing is given to thought, how can a nothing, an empty space, 'appear'? Is there not here something like a trace of that fundamental status of the transcendental imagination as an originary source of knowledge beyond the sundering of understanding and sensibility, receptivity and spontaneity which Kant, according to Heidegger, hastened to cover up in the second edition of the *Critique*? Why do the ice floes on the verge of liquefaction, which Kant evoked in his topographic sketch of the land of truth, never melt?

To try to respond to these questions, I would like to dwell on the classificatory table of the forms of the concept of nothingness that closes the Transcendental Analytic. This table looks like one of those outmoded scholastic exercises that do not seem to present thinking with any substantive problem. This is perhaps why Heidegger, in whose thought the concept of nothing occupies a central place, barely dwells on this table. And yet, inapparent and insubstantial as it may seem, this table contains a decisive problem. Kant distinguishes four determinations of the nothing, two positive, so to speak, and two negative:

NOTHING,

as

1.

Empty concept without object,
ens rationis.

2.	3.
Empty object of	Empty intuition
a concept,	without an object,
nihil privativum.	*ens imaginarium.*

4.

Empty object without concept,
nihil negativum.[8]

Numbers 2 and 4 are not problematic: the *nihil privativum* is simply negation, namely, 'a concept of the absence of an object, such as a shadow or cold', while the *nihil negativum* is the object of a concept that contradicts itself, 'like a rectilinear figure with two sides.'[9] We need to pause instead on numbers 1 and 3, the *ens rationis* and the *ens imaginarium*, which are clearly the more significant ones for Kant. The first is a concept to which no object corresponds, such

8 Kant, *Critique of Pure Reason*, p. 383 (A292/B348).

9 Kant, *Critique of Pure Reason*, p. 382 (A291/B347).

as the thing in itself and the noumenon. Examples of the *ens imaginarium* are instead pure space and pure time, simple forms of intuition without substance. The first, Kant writes, are *leere Begriffe*, empty concepts in which nothing is really thought, the second are instead *leere Data zu Begriffen*. This latter expression—'data empty for concepts' [*dati vuoti ai concetti*]—is so singular that the translators of the 1910 Italian edition, Giovanni Gentile and Giuseppe Lombardo Radice, made a translation mistake, which has obstinately survived in all subsequent editions and revisions: they translated it as 'empty data of concepts' [*vuoti dati di concetti*]. Faced with the paradox of the givenness [*darsi*] of an emptiness to concepts and thought—as the German text unequivocally reads—they retreated just like, according to Heidegger, Kant would have retreated faced with abyss of the transcendental imagination.

The problematic status of these two figures of the nothing appears here in full light. How can we think an empty givenness, the givenness of a void in the *ens imaginarium*? And, as for the *ens rationis*, what does a thought that thinks nothing think? We have here, on the one hand, a receptivity, an intuition that presents us only with an emptiness and, on the other, a spontaneity, a thinking in which nothing is thought.

The necessary union of the two *Grundquellen*, of the two originary sources of knowledge—receptivity and spontaneity—which constituted the cornerstone of the *Critique*, here seems to fracture. And, in this break, it is as though there negatively appeared that other source of knowledge, the transcendental imagination, which had been deleted from the second edition of the work. Heidegger's interpretation of Kant would thus find further confirmation: there is, prior to sensibility and the understanding, a receptivity that presents nothing, just as there is a thought that thinks nothing. And it is over this nothing that stretches the inextinguishable appearance of the Transcendental Dialectic.

I would now like to show how Kant never really stopped interrogating himself over the paradoxical status of these two figures of the nothing, and how the thinking of his final years was instead nothing but an obsessive, almost fevered meditation of this problem. Before examining the re-emergence of this motif in the *Opus Postumum*, I would like to pause briefly on the section of the *Critique of the Power of Judgement* that bears the title 'Analytic of the Sublime'. I have chosen the 'Analytic of the Sublime' because the problem appears within it in particularly drastic terms, but I think that the whole of the third *Critique* allows for a reading in this direction. Kant defines the sublime as a representation 'which determines the mind to think of the unattainability of nature as a presentation of ideas,'[10] and

10 Immanuel Kant, *Critique of the Power of Judgement* (Paul Guyer ed.)

he is careful to note that, since ideas cannot in any case be exhibited, the effort of representation is here necessarily in vain. But this effort, Kant adds, 'and the feeling of the unattainability of the idea by means of the imagination [...] compels us to think nature itself in its totality, as the presentation of something supersensible, subjectively, without being able to produce this presentation objectively'.[11]

In the experience of the sublime—if we can indeed speak of an experience here—the imagination is indeed led beyond its limits but in its momentum 'finds nothing beyond the sensible to which it can attach itself.'[12] Kant insists repeatedly on the fact that here 'the senses no longer see anything before them.'[13] Sublime presentation is thus purely negative: *nothing* is properly exhibited within it. Jean-Luc Nancy is right, in a recent study on the Analytic of the Sublime, to write that 'presentation does indeed take place, but [...] it does not *present* anything. Pure presentation (presentation of presentation itself) or presentation of the totality, presents nothing at all.'[14] I believe that these necessarily brief observations nonetheless allow us to glean

---

(Cambridge: Cambridge University Press, 2000), p. 151.

11 Kant, *Critique of the Power of Judgement*, p. 151.

12 Kant, *Critique of the Power of Judgement*, p. 156.

13 Kant, *Critique of the Power of Judgement*, p. 156.

14 Jean-Luc Nancy, 'The Sublime Offering' in Jean-François Courtine et al., *Of the Sublime: Presence in Question* (Jeffrey S. Librett trans.) (Albany, NY: State University of New York Press, 1993), p. 47.

the analogy between the negative exhibition that is at stake in the sublime and the 'givenness of a void' of the *ens imaginarium*. But, once again, Kant does not fully explain how it is possible to think a purely negative exhibition.

It is in the *Opus Postumum* that the problem which had remained unresolved in the *Critique* is reprised and, if not solved, at least given its most extreme and deliberate formulation. A few words first on this unfinished text, to which Kant sometimes refers to as his most important work and which has remained a Cinderella of sorts among Kant's great works—the only one for which the bibliography, albeit substantial, is not vast. There is an Italian translation of it by Vittorio Mathieu, from Volumes 21 and 22 of the Academie Ausgabe, which has the great merit of having systematically arranged the cumbersome material of the manuscripts. But the fact that Mathieu's exegesis is especially oriented towards the problem of the passage from metaphysics to physics hindered him from grasping all the implications of Kant's final effort.

In the *Opus Postumum*, Kant starts precisely from those *leere Data*, from that empty givenness to concepts which is at stake in the *ens imaginarium*, that is to say in pure space and pure time, and from those apparently empty concepts that are the noumenon and the concepts of force, ether and matter, which cannot be experienced and yet were taken to exist by the physics of his time. In other words, he is again thinking of that division of knowledge into two fundamental sources that constituted one of the essential presuppositions of the *Critique*. In the first, an object is given to us, in the second it is thought in relation to representation. The cornerstone of critique was that knowledge can only stem from the union of these originary sources. But now Kant asks himself: how is an 'empty givenness' possible then, such as we find in the *ens imaginarium*, in pure space and pure time? And how is an empty thinking possible? What is at stake in a receptivity without object and a spontaneity which in itself is empty? Pure space and time, noumenon, matter and gravitational forces confront Kant with a claim to consistency that can no longer be dispelled through the idea of *Schein*, of transcendental appearance. In effect, this idea entirely falls away in the *Opus Postumum*, save for one point, where the text makes room for a new concept which, to our mind, is of central importance for the interpretation of the last Kant, namely, that of 'phenomenon of the phenomenon' (*Erscheinung einer Erscheinung*), the appearance of appearance itself.

With a nigh-on maniacal repetitiousness, Kant once again puts into question the status of pure space and pure time, which the *Critique* seemed to have settled definitively. An example among the countless almost identical ones that fill the pages of fascicles VII and XI:

Space and time are not *objects* of intuition. For
were they objects of intuition, they would be real
things and require, in turn, another intuition in
order to be represented to one as objects, and so
on to infinity. Intuitions are not perceptions (that
is, empirical) if they are pure, for that requires
forces which determine the senses. How is it possible, however, that pure intuitions yield, at the
same time, principles of perception—e.g. the
attraction of cosmic bodies? [Space and time are
not *objects* of intuition] but, rather, subjective
forms of intuition itself, insofar as they contain a
principle of synthetic a priori propositions and of
the possibility of a transcendental philosophy;
[they contain] phenomena prior to all perceptions
[*Erscheinungen vor allen Wahrnehmungen*].[15]

I would like to draw your attention to this paradoxical
expression, which within the parameters of the first *Critique*
is meaningless: 'phenomena prior to all perceptions'. We
have here a phenomenal dimension that precedes every
concrete experience, almost as though something like a
phenomenality could be given prior to sensible experience,
before phenomena themselves. Kant's notes relentlessly
repeat that space and time are not only forms of intuition,
but themselves intuitions, even if it remains unclear what

15 Kant, *Opus Postumum* (Förster and Rosen trans), p. 159 [translation
modified; Förster and Rosen render *Erscheinungen* as 'appearances' —
Trans.].

is intuited within them, given that, as pure intuitions, they are by definition devoid of an object, even if we posit something like a matter within them. Thus, Kant can write the following about empty space:

> There can be no experience of empty space, nor can it be inferred as an object of experience. In order to be apprised of the existence of a matter, I require the influence of a matter on my senses. Thus the proposition: 'There are empty spaces' can be neither a mediate nor an immediate proposition of experience; it is, rather, merely ratiocinative [*vernünfelt*].[16]

The problem that Kant is wrestling with here is that of the status of that originary source of knowledge that is receptivity, a status which in the *Critique* did not appear as problematic. How can there be something like a 'source' and how can we think a pure receptivity, that is to say, a phenomenality prior to every phenomenon? If space and time, as imaginary entities, are a pure nothing, mere empty ratiocination, why do they not remain empty but instead offer principles to perception, like matter and gravitational forces?

This is why, in the *Opus Postumum*, Kant affirms with such resoluteness the existence of the ether, namely, sensible full space, a kind of matter anterior to every sensible body, which lies at the foundation of every possible experience. The existence of the ether is in no way for Kant a fact of

---

16 Kant, *Opus Postumum* (Förster and Rosen trans), pp. 67–68.

experience, but this does not mean that it is simply hypo-thetical. It is, in some sense, a truly inevitable appearance, an absolutely necessary *ens rationis*, in which something is not simply thought but, without being experienced, nevertheless *gives itself* to thought. With a formula that from the standpoint of the *Critique* would be simply non-sensical, Kant writes that the ether is 'space made percep-tible, yet given not to the senses, but to thought'.

So, something is given in the empty givenness of pure space and time as *entia imaginaria*, just as something is thought in those *entia rationis* which are the thing in itself, ether and matter. But what?

It is here that Kant advances the idea of a 'phenomenon of the phenomenon [*Erscheinung einer Erscheinung*]', which I would like as far as possible to clarify. In space and time as pure intuitions, in the ether as pure space made percep-tible or in the thing in itself, we are not dealing with phe-nomena, but with the manner in which the subject, in the phenomenon, is affected not by the object, but by itself, by its own receptivity. 'The phenomenon of the phenomenon,' Kant writes, 'is a representation of the formal with which the subject affects itself and is spontaneously an object for itself.'[17] On another sheet, we read that the 'phenomenon of the phenomenon [. . .] is the phenomenon of the self-affecting subject.'[18] This is repeated for the thing in itself,

17 I could not locate this passage in the English edition of the *Opus Postumum*. [Trans.]

for which Kant seems to provide a definition that sounds surprisingly Nietzschean: 'The thing in itself is not another object, but another relation of representation to the same object [. . .] The *ens rationis* = x is self-positing according to the principle of identity, in which the subject is thought as self-affecting, and therefore, in its form only as phenomenon.'[19] At the foundation of the givenness of a pure receptivity there is a self-affection. The originary source of knowledge is not a datum that can be interrogated *a priori* but rather—and here lies the novelty of the *Opus Postumum*—something that constitutively possesses the form of a self-affection, which coincides with the very possibility of knowledge.

---

18 Kant, *Opus Postumum* (Förster and Rosen trans), p. 117 [translation modified: where Agamben gives 'phenomenon of the phenomenon', Förster and Rosen have 'appearance of the appearance' —Trans.].

19 I could not locate this passage in the English edition of the *Opus Postumum*, where some related formulae can nonetheless be found: 'space and time [. . .] are mere appearances, that is, representations which relate to the object of intuition insofar as [the subject] is affected by it, and are the subjective element of the subject's self-affection (formally)' (p. 174); 'the concept of a thing in itself is merely a thought-object (*ens rationis*) and serves as an object = x in order to represent the object of intuition in contrast to appearance. The thing in itself is not something given (*dabile*) but what is thought merely as corresponding (notwithstanding that it remains absent), belonging to the division. It stands only like a cipher [*Ziffer*]' (p. 176); 'The thing in itself is a thought-object (*ens rationis*) of the connection of this manifold whole into the unity to which the subject constitutes itself. The object in itself = x is the sense-object *in itself*; but as another mode of representation, not as another object' (pp. 179–80). [Trans.]

We can perhaps now try to answer the question we've repeatedly asked ourselves during the course of this lecture, about the empty givenness of the *ens imaginarium* and the empty thinking of the *ens rationis*. What is given in that empty givenness, what is thought in that empty thinking are the same thing, namely, a pure self-affection. In it the subject is affected by itself, it suffers its own receptivity and, in this way, becomes 'impassioned' in the etymological sense of the term, that is to say, it feels itself and gives itself to itself while opening itself up to the world. A passage from the *Opus Postumum* expressed the nature of this original gift in a formula wherein the meaning of the Kantian doctrine of the two sources of knowledge is utterly transfigured: 'Intuition and concept belong to knowledge: that I am given to myself and thought by myself as object. Something exists (*apprehensio simplex*); I am not merely logical subject and predicate, but also object of *perception* (*dabile non solum cogitabile*).'[20] In pure self-affection, in this gift of oneself to oneself, the two originary sources of knowledge coincide with no remainder. Pure passivity and pure spontaneity coincide in the passion of self. A note confirms this beyond any doubt: 'Positing and perception, spontaneity and receptivity, the objective and subjective relation, are simultaneous [*zugleich*]; because they are identical . . . as appearances of how the subject is affected—thus are given in the same *actus*.'[21] This self-affection, this

---

20 Kant, *Opus Postumum* (Förster and Rosen trans), pp. 194–95.

21 Kant, *Opus Postumum* (Förster and Rosen trans), p. 132.

coming to appearance of appearing itself, is the abyss into which now plunge, as into in their common spring, the two originary sources of knowledge.

If we now return to the concept of inextinguishable appearance with which we began, we see that what the first *Critique* presented as an illusion here becomes self-affection which, more originary than spontaneity or receptivity, is at the foundation of every knowledge. 'The phenomenon of the phenomenon,' as another note unequivocally asserts, 'is appearance, namely, semblance [*die Apparenz, das ist der Schein*].'[22]

Appearance is therefore truly inextinguishable: the voyager can never reach its end, because what is at stake within appearance is the very fount of knowledge, the subject's pure giving itself to itself. The topography of the island of truth is really more complicated than it seemed. The Heideggerian interpretation, which looked for a more originary opening in the transcendental imagination, hit the target in this respect; however, faced with the abyss of this fount, Kant did not ultimately retreat; on the contrary, in his final years he thought it in all its aporetic character. And I believe that only this paradoxical concept of an originary passion of self, in which nothing is given but givenness itself, could provide the proper site for an aesthetics that wished radically to think Kant with Heidegger.

22 I could not locate this passage in the English edition of the *Opus Postumum*. [Trans.]

BIBLIOGRAPHY

ADORNO, Theodor W. *Negative Dialectics* (E. B. Ashton trans.). London: Routledge, 1973.

AGAMBEN, Giorgio, and Jean-Baptiste Brenet. *Intellect d'amour*. Lagrasse: Verdier, 2018.

——. *Opus Dei: An Archaeology of Duty* (Adam Kotsko trans.). Stanford, CA: Stanford University Press, 2013.

——. *The Use of Bodies: Homo Sacer IV, 2* (Adam Kotsko trans.). Stanford, CA: Stanford University Press, 2016.

ALBERTUS Magnus. *Commentarii in Sententiarum* in *Opera omnia*, VOL. 25 (Auguste Borgnet ed.). Paris, 1893.

ALEXANDER OF APHRODISIAS. *In Aristotelis Topicorum: Libros Octo Commentaria* (Max Wallies ed.). Commentaria in Aristotelem Graeca, VOL. 2, part 2. Berlin: Reimer, 1891.

——. *Quaestiones 1.1–2.15* (R. W. Sharples trans.). Ancient Commentators on Aristotle (Richard Sorabji series ed.). London: Bloomsbury, 2014.

ALIGHIERI, Dante. *The Divine Comedy, Volume 2: Purgatory* (Mark Musa trans.). London: Penguin, 1985.

——. *Monarchy* (Prue Shaw trans. and ed.). Cambridge: Cambridge University Press, 1996.

ANSELM OF CANTERBURY. *Fidens quaerens intellectum* (Alexandre Koyré ed.). Paris: Vrin, 1982.

APULEIUS. *On the Doctrines of the Philosophy of Plato* in *The Metamorphosis, or Golden Ass, and Philosophical Works* (Thomas Taylor trans.). London: Robert Triphook and Thomas Rodd, 1822.

AQUINAS, Thomas. *Summa Theologica*, VOL. 1 (Fathers of the English Dominican Province and Daniel J. Sullivan trans). Chicago, IL: Encyclopaedia Britannica, 1923.

ARISTOTLE. *Categories and De Interpretatione* (J. L. Ackrill trans.). Oxford: Clarendon Press, 1963.

———. *De Anima* (Christopher Shields trans.). Oxford: Clarendon Press, 2016.

———. *Metaphysics* (Richard Hope trans.). Ann Arbor: University of Michigan Press, 1960.

———. *Physics: Books I and II* (William Charlton trans. and ed.). Oxford: Clarendon Books, 1992.

———. *Physics: Books III and IV* (Edward Hussey trans. and ed.). Oxford: Clarendon Press, 1983.

AUGUSTINE OF HIPPO. *On Christian Doctrine* (J. F. Shaw trans.). Mineola, NY: Dover, 2009.

———. *Tractates on the Gospel of John 1–10* (John W. Rettig trans.). Washington, DC: The Catholic University of America Press, 1988.

AVICENNA. *Liber de philosophia prima* (S. Van Riet ed.). Leiden: Brill, 1977.

BARDOUT, Jean-Christophe. 'Note sur les significations cartésiennes de la réalité'. *Quaestio* 17 (2017).

BAUMGARTEN, Alexander Gottlieb. *Metaphysica*. Halle, 1739.

———. *Metaphysics: A Critical Translation with Kant's Elucidations, Selected Notes and Related Materials* (Courtney D. Fugate and John Hymers trans and eds). London: Bloomsbury, 2013.

BENJAMIN, Walter. 'Theological-Political Fragment' in *Selected Writings: Volume 3, 1935–1938* (Howard Eiland and Michael W. Jennings eds, Edmund Jephcott, Howard Eiland et al. trans). Cambridge, MA: Harvard University Press, 2002.

BENVENISTE, Émile. *Problems in General Linguistics* (Mary Elizabeth Meek trans.). Coral Gables, FL: University of Miami Press, 1971.

BERGSON, Henri. 'The Possible and the Real' in *Key Writings* (Keith Ansell Pearson and John Mullarkey eds). London: Continuum, 2002.

BOEHM, Rudolph. *Das Grundlegende und das Wesentliche*. The Hague: Martinus Nijhoff, 1965.

BOULNOIS, Olivier. 'L'invention de la réalité'. *Quaestio* 17 (2017).

BRADWARDINE, Thomas. *Thomae Bradwardini* [...] *De causa Dei contra Pelagium* [...] *libri tres.* London, 1618.

BRISSON, Luc. *Le même et l'autre dans la structure ontologique du 'Timée' de Platon.* Paris: Klincksieck, 1974.

CALCIDIUS. *Commentario al 'Timeo' di Platone* (Claudio Moreschini ed.). Milan: Bompiani, 2003.

———. *On Plato's 'Timaeus'* (John Magee trans. and ed.). Cambridge, MA: Harvard University Press, 2016.

———. *Timaeus a Calcidio translatus commentarioque instructus* (J. H. Waszink ed.). Plato Latinus, VOL. 4. London: Warburg Institute, 1962.

CHAUVIN, Étienne. *Thesaurus philosophicus.* Rotterdam: Pieter van der Slaart, 1692.

CICERO. *Brutus. Orator* (G. L. Hendrickson and H. M. Hubbell trans). Cambridge, MA: Harvard University Press, 1971.

———. *On the Nature of the Gods. Academics* (H. Rackham trans.). Cambridge, MA: Harvard University Press, 1933.

———. *On the Orator: Book 3. On Fate. Stoic Paradoxes. Divisions of Oratory* (H. Rackham trans.). Cambridge, MA: Harvard University Press, 1942.

———. *Topics in On Invention. The Best Kind of Orator. Topics* (H. M. Hubbell trans.). Cambridge, MA: Harvard University Press, 1949.

COURTINE, Jean-François. *Suarez et le système de la métaphysique.* Paris: Presses universitaires de France, 1990.

D'ALVERNY, Marie-Thérèse. 'L'Introduction d'Avicenne en Occident'. *La revue du Caire, Millenaire d'Avicenna* (special issue) (1951): 130–39.

DAGRON, Tristan. 'David of Dinant—On the Quaternuli Fragment <Hyle, Mens, Deus>'. *Revue de métaphysique et de morale* 4(40) (2003): 419–436.

DE RIJK, Lambertus Marie. *Logica modernorum: A Contribution to the History of Early Terminist Logic, Volume 2: Part One, The Origin and Early Development of the Theory of Supposition.* Assen: Van Gorcum & Company, 1967.

DERRIDA, Jacques. 'How to Avoid Speaking: Denials' (Ken Frieden trans.) in *Derrida and Negative Theology* (Harold Coward and Toby Foshay eds). Albany, NY: State University of New York Press, 1992.

——. 'Khōra' (Ian McLeod trans.) in *On the Name* (Thomas Dutoit ed.). Stanford, CA: Stanford University Press, 1995.

——. 'We Other Greeks' (Pascale-Anne Brault and Michael Naas trans) in *Derrida and Antiquity* (Miriam Leonard ed.). Oxford: Oxford University Press, 2010.

——. *Rogues: Two Essays on Reason* (Pascale-Anne Brault and Michael Naas trans). Stanford, CA: Stanford University Press, 2005.

DESCARTES, René. *Les méditations métaphysiques*. Paris: The widow of Jean Camusat and Pierre Le Petit, 1647.

——. *Meditations on First Philosophy* (Michael Moriarty trans.). Oxford: Oxford University Press, 2008.

——. *The Philosophical Works of Descartes*, VOL. 2 (Elizabeth S. Haldane and G. R. T. Ross trans). New York: Dover, 1934.

DESMAIZEAUX, Pierre. 'Article II. Lettre de Mr. Des Maizeaux à l'Auteur de ces Nouvelles'. *Nouvelles de la republique des lettres* (November 1701): 510–519.

DIANO, Carlo. 'Il problema della materia in Platone: la chora del Timeo'. *Giornale critico della filosofia italiana* 49 (1979): 321–35.

——. *Studi e saggi di filosofia antica*. Padua: Antenore, 1973.

DINANT, David di. *Mente Materia Dio / Mens Hyle Deus* (Emanuele Dattilo ed.). Genoa: Il nuovo melangolo, 2022.

DUHEM, Pierre. *Système du monde: Histoire des doctrines cosmologiques de Platon à Copernic*, VOL. I. Paris: Hermann, 1913.

EL-BIZRI, Nader. 'On KAI XΩPA: Situating Heidegger Between the Sophist and the Timaeus'. *Studia Phaenomenologica* 4(1–2) (2004): 73–98.

ESPOSITO, Costantino. 'L'impossibilità come trascendentale: Per una storia del concetto di impossibile da Suárez a Heidegger'. *Archivio di filosofia* 78(1) (2010).

FOUCAULT, Michel. *The Government of Self and Others*: Lectures at the Collège de France, 1982–1983 (Graham Burchell trans., Frédéric Gros ed.). Basingstoke: Palgrave Macmillan, 2010.

FRANCIS OF MARCHIA. 'Questiones in Metaphysicam, I, q. I' in Albert Zimmerman (ed.), *Ontologie oder Metaphysik: Die Diskussion über den Gegenstand in Metaphysik im 13 und 14 Jahrhundert*. Leuven: Peeters, 1998.

FRANCIS OF MEYRONNES. *Tractatus formalitatum* in *In Libros Sententiarum, Quodlibeta, Tractatus formalitatum, De primo principio, Terminorum theologicalium declarationes, De univocatione* (Mauritius de Hibernia ed.). Venice, 1520.

FUJISAWA, Norio. 'Ἔχειν, Μετἠχειν, and Idioms of "Paradeigmatism" in Plato's Theory of Forms'. *Phronesis* 19 (1974): 30–57.

GAUVIN, Joseph. 'Les dérivés de "Res" dans la Phénomenologie de l'esprit' in Marta Fattori and Massimo Luigi Bianchi (eds), *Res: III Colloquio Internazionale del Lessico Intellettuale Europeo (Roma, 7–9 gennaio 1980)*. Rome: Edizioni dell'Ateneo, 1982.

GILES OF ROME. *In Secundum Librum Sententiarum Quaestiones*, part 1. Venice: Zilletus, 1581.

GILSON, Étienne. *L'Être et l'essence*. 3rd edn. Paris: Vrin, 2000.

GRAHAM, A. C. 'Being in Linguistics and Philosophy: A Preliminary Inquiry.' *Foundations of Language* 1 (1965): 223–31.

GROSSETESTE, Robert. *On Light* (Clare C. Riedl trans. and ed.). Milwaukee: Marquette University Press, 1942.

HAMESSE, Jacqueline. 'Res chez les auteurs philosophiques des XII et XIII siècles ou le passage de la neutralité à la specificité' in Marta Fattori and Massimo Luigi Bianchi (eds), *Res: III Colloquio Internazionale del Lessico Intellettuale Europeo (Roma, 7–9 gennaio 1980)*. Rome: Edizioni dell'Ateneo, 1982.

HAPP, Heinz. *Hyle: Studien zum aristotelischen Materie-Begriff*. Berlin and New York: De Gruyter, 1971.

HEGEL, G. W. F. *Lectures on the History of Philosophy, Volume 2: Plato and the Platonists* (E. S. Haldane and Frances H. Simson trans). Lincoln, NE, and London: University of Nebraska Press, 1995.

——. *The Phenomenology of Spirit* (Terry Pinkard trans. and ed.). Cambridge: Cambridge University Press, 2018.

HEIDEGGER, Martin. 'The Thing' in *Poetry, Language, Thought* (Albert Hofstadter trans.). New York: Harper & Row, 1971.

——. *Being and Time* (John Macquarrie and Edward Robinson eds). Oxford: Blackwell, 1962.

——. *Contributions to Philosophy (Of the Event)* (Richard Rojcewicz and Daniela Vallega-Neu trans). Bloomington, IN: Indiana University Press, 2012.

——. *Discourse on Thinking: A Translation of Gelassenheit* (John M. Anderson and E. Hans Freund trans). New York: Harper & Row, 1966.

——. *Four Seminars* (Andrew J. Mitchell and François Raffoul trans). Bloomington, IN: Indiana University Press, 2003.

——. *Heraclitus: The Inception of Occidental Thinking / Logic: Heraclitus' Doctrine of the Logos* (Julia Goesser Assaiante and S. Montgomery Ewegen trans). London: Bloomsbury, 2018.

——. *Introduction to Metaphysics* (Gregory Fried and Richard Polt trans). New Haven, CT: Yale University Press, 2000.

——. *Kant and the Problem of Metaphysics*. 5th edn (Richard Taft trans.). Bloomington, IN: Indiana University Press, 1997.

HENRY OF GHENT. *Quodlibet VII* (G. A. Wilson ed.). Opera Omnia, VOL. 11. Leuven: Leuven University Press, 1991.

HÖLDERLIN, Friedrich. 'Anmerkung zum Oedipus' in *Hölderlin Sämtliche Werke*, VOL. 5 (F. Beissner ed.). Stuttgart: Kohlhammer, 1954.

HOPKINS, Jasper. *Nicholas of Cusa on God as Not-other: A Translation and an Appraisal of 'De Li Non Aliud'*. Minneapolis: University of Minnesota Press, 1979.

ISAR, Nicoletta. 'Chôra: Tracing the Presence'. *Review of European Studies* 1(1) (2009).

JOLIVET, Jean. 'Aux origins de l'ontologie d'Ibn Sina' in *Philosophie médiévale arabe et latine*. Paris: Vrin, 1995.

KANT, Immanuel. *Critique of Pure Reason* (Paul Guyer and Allen W. Wood trans and eds). Cambridge: Cambridge University Press, 1998.

——. *Critique of the Power of Judgement* (Paul Guyer ed.). Cambridge: Cambridge University Press, 2000.

——. 'The Only Possible Argument in Support of a Demonstration of the Existence of God (1763)' in *Theoretical Philosophy, 1755–1770* (David Walford with Ralf Meerbote trans and eds). Cambridge: Cambridge University Press, 1992.

——. *Opus Postumum* (Eckart Förster and Michael Rosen trans, Eckart Förster ed.). Cambridge: Cambridge University Press, 1993.

KLEIN, Robert. 'The Eclipse of the Work of Art' in *Form and Meaning: Writings on the Renaissance and Modern Art* (Madeline Jay and Leon Wieseltier trans). Princeton, NJ: Princeton University Press, 1981.

KOYRÉ, Alexandre. *Études d'histoire de la pensée philosophique*. Paris: Gallimard, 1971.

LAMPERT, Laurence, and Christopher Planeaux. 'Who's Who in Plato's Timaeus-Critias and Why'. *Review of Metaphysics* 52(1) (1998): 87–125.

LEIBNIZ, Gottfried Wilhelm. *De ratione cur haec existant potius quam alia* in *Sämtliche Schriften und Briefe, Philosophische Schriften*, VOL. 6 (Heinrich Schepers ed.). Berlin: Akademie Verlag, 1990.

——. *Die philosophischen Schitften von Gottfried Wilhelm Leibniz* (Carl Immanuel Gerhardt ed.). Berlin: Weidmannsche Buchhandlung, 1878–90.

——, and Samuel Clarke. *Correspondence* (Roger Ariew ed.). Indianapolis, IN, and Cambridge: Hackett, 2020.

——, and Samuel Clarke. *The Leibniz–Clarke Correspondence* (H. G. Alexander ed.). Manchester: Manchester University Press, 1956.

LEOPARDI, Giacomo. *Pensieri di varia filosofia e di bella letteratura (Zibaldone di pensieri)*, VOL. 2. Florence: Successori Le Monnier, 1898.

LIZZINI, Olga. 'Wuḍūd-Mawḍūd / Existence-Existent in Avicenna: A Key Ontological Notion in Arabic Philosophy'. *Quaestio* 3 (2003).

LOVEJOY, Arthur O. *The Great Chain of Being: A Study of the History of an Idea*. New edn. New Brunswick, NJ, and London: Transaction Publishers, 2009 [1936].

LUCRETIUS. *Of the Nature of Things: A Metrical Translation* (William Ellery Leonard trans.). London, Paris and Toronto: J. M. Dent & Sons Ltd, 1916.

MAJORANA, Ettore. 'Il valore delle leggi statistiche nella fisica e nelle scienze sociali' (1934) in *Che cos'è reale?* (Giorgio Agamben ed.). Vicenza: Neri Pozza, 2016.

MARX, Karl, and Frederick Engels. *Collected Works, Volume 1: Marx, 1835–1843*. London: Lawrence and Wishart, 1975.

MARX, Karl. *Early Writings* (Rodney Livingstone and Gregor Benton trans). London: Penguin, 1992.

MICRAELIUS, Johannes. *Lexicon philosophicum terminorum philosophis usitatorum*. 2nd edn. Szczecin: Jeremiah Mamphras, 1661 [1653].

MORE, Henry. 'An Appendix to the Foregoing Antidote against Atheism' in *A Collection of Several Philosophical Writings*. London: J. Flesher, 1662.

———. *Enchiridion Metaphysicum sive de rebus incorporis, per H. More Cantabrigiensem*. London: E. Flesher, 1671.

———. *The Immortality of the Soul* (A. Jacob ed.). Dordrecht: Martinus Nijhoff, 1987 [1662].

NANCY, Jean-Luc. 'The Sublime Offering' in Jean-François Courtine et al., *Of the Sublime: Presence in Question* (Jeffrey S. Librett trans.). Albany, NY: State University of New York Press, 1993.

NEWTON, Isaac. *Opticks, or, A Treatise of the Reflections, Refractions, Inflections & Colours of Light*. New York: Dover, 1952.

———. *Philosophical Writings* (Andrew Janiak ed.). Cambridge: Cambridge University Press, 2004.

———. *Trialogus De Possest*. Paris: Vrin, 2006.

Nɪᴋᴇᴘʜᴏʀᴏs. *Antirrhetikos* in Jacques Paul Migne (ed.), *Patrologia Graeca*, ᴠᴏʟ. 100. Paris: Imprimerie Catholique, 1865.

———. *Expositio in canonem missae* in *Patrologia Latina*, ᴠᴏʟ. 160 (Jacques-Paul Migne ed.). Paris: Garnier, 1880.

Pᴀsǫᴜᴀʟɪ, Giorgio. *Le lettere di Platone*. Florence: Le Monnier, 1938; 2nd edn: Florence: Sansoni, 1967.

Pʟᴀᴛᴏ. *Complete Works* (John M. Cooper and D. S. Hutchinson eds). Indianapolis, IN, and Cambridge: Hackett, 1997.

———. *Phaedrus and Letters VII and VIII* (Walter Hamilton trans.). London: Penguin, 1973.

———. *Timaeus* (Donald J. Zeyl trans.). Indianapolis, IN: Hackett, 2020.

Pʟᴏᴛɪɴᴜs. *Ennead II.4: On Matter* (A. A. Long trans. and ed.). Las Vegas, NV: Parmenides, 2022.

———. *Ennead*, ᴠᴏʟ. 3 (A. H. Armstrong trans.). Cambridge, MA: Harvard University Press, 1967.

Pʀᴀᴅᴇᴀᴜ, Jean-François. 'Être quelque part, occupier une place: ΤΟΠΟΣ et ΧΩPA dans le Timée'. *Les Études philosophiques* 3 (1995): 375–400.

Pʀᴏᴄʟᴜs. *Commentary on Plato's 'Timaeus', Volume I, Book 1: Proclus on the Socratic State and Atlantis* (Harold Tarrant trans. and ed.). Cambridge: Cambridge University Press, 2010.

———. *Commentary on Plato's 'Timaeus', Volume II, Book 2: Proclus on the Causes of the Cosmos and its Creation* (David T. Runia and Michael Share trans and eds). Cambridge: Cambridge University Press, 2008.

Qᴜɪɴᴛɪʟɪᴀɴ. *The Orator's Education, Volume IV: Books 9–10* (Donald A. Russell trans. and ed.). Cambridge, MA: Harvard University Press, 2002.

Rɪᴛᴛᴇʀ, Constantin. 'Timaios cap. I'. *Philologus* 62(1) (1903): 410–18.

Rɪᴠᴀᴜᴅ, Albert. *Introduction to Plato, Timée, Critias*. Paris: Les Belles Lettres, 1963.

Sᴀʟʟɪs, John. 'Last Words: Generosity and Reserve'. *Mosaic* 39(3) (2006).

Sᴄʜüʀᴍᴀɴɴ, Reiner. *Heidegger on Being and Acting: From Principles to Anarchy* (Christine-Marie Gros trans.). Bloomington, IN: Indiana University Press, 1990.

Scotus, John Duns. *Contingency and Freedom: Lectura I 39* (A. Vos Jaczn, H. Veldhuis, A. H. Looman-Graaskamp, E. Dekker and N. W. Den Bok trans and eds). Dordrecht: Kluwer, 1994.

——. *The De Primo Principio of John Duns Scotus* (Evan Roche trans.). St Bonaventure, NY: The Franciscan Institute, 1949.

Siger de Brabant. *Quaestiones in tertium de anima* (Bernardo Carlos Bazán ed.). Louvain and Paris: Publications Universitaires, 1972.

——. *Quaestiones in Metaphysicam* (Armand Maurer ed.). Louvain-la-Neuve: Institut supérieur de philosophie, 1983.

Silvestris, Bernardus. *Cosmografia e Commento a Marziano Capella* in *Thierry of Chartres, William of Conches and Bernardus Silvestris, Il divino e il megacosmo: Testi filosofici e scientifici della scuola di Chartres* (Enzo Maccagnolo ed.). Milan: Rusconi, 1980.

——. *Cosmographia* (Winthrop Wetherbee trans. and ed.). New York: Columbia University Press, 1990.

Simplicius. *On Aristotle Physics 1.5–9* (Hans Baltussen, Michael Atkinson, Michael Share and Ian Mueller trans). Ancient Commentators on Aristotle (Richard Sorabji series ed.). London: Bloomsbury, 2014.

——. *On Aristotle Physics 4.1–5 and 10–14* (J. O. Urmson trans.). Ancient Commentators on Aristotle (Richard Sorabji series ed.). London: Bloomsbury, 2014.

——. *In Aristotelis Physicorum libros quattuor priores commentaria*, vol. 1 (Hermann Diels ed.). Berlin: G. Reimeri, 1882.

Spinoza, Baruch. *The Ethics* in *The Spinoza Reader: The Ethics and Other Works* (Edwin Curley trans. and ed.). Princeton, NJ: Princeton University Press, 1994.

——. *Principles of Cartesian Philosophy* (Harry E. Wedeck trans.). London: Peter Owen Ltd, 1961.

Stocks, J. L. 'The Divided Line of Plato Rep. VI'. *The Classical Quarterly* 5(2) (1911).

Suárez, Francisco. *Metaphysical Disputation II: On the Essential Concept or Concept of Being* (Shane Duarte trans. and ed.). Washington, DC: The Catholic University of America, 2023.

TAGLIA, Angelica. *Il concetto di pistis in Platone*. Rome: Le Lettere, 1998.

THEOPHRASTUS. *Métaphysique* (André Laks and Glenn W. Most trans and eds). Paris: Les Belles Lettres, 1993.

VALENTE, Luisa. 'Ens, unum, bonum: Elementi per una storia dei trascendentali in Boezio e nella tradizione boeziana del sec. XII' in Stefano Caroti, Ruedi Imbach, Zénon Kaluza, Loris Sturlese and Giorgio Stabile (eds), *'Ad ingenii acuitionem': Studies in Honour of Alfonso Maierù*. Louvain-la-Neuve: Brepols, 2006.

VARRO. *On the Latin Language* (Roland G. Kent trans.). London: William Heinemann Ltd, 1938.

VASILIU, Anca. *Du diaphane: Image, milieu, lumière dans la pensée antique et médiévale*. Paris: Vrin, 1997.

WEIL, Simone. 'Classical Science and After' in *On Science, Necessity, and the Love of God* (Richard Ress trans. and ed.). Oxford: Oxford University Press, 1968.

WISNOVSKY, Robert. 'Notes on Avicenna's Concept of Thingness (šay'iyya)'. *Arabic Sciences and Philosophy* 10 (2000).

WITTGENSTEIN, Ludwig. *Tractatus Logico-Philosophicus* (D. F. Pears and B. F. McGuinness trans). London: Routledge, 2001.

WOLFF, Christian Freiherr von. *Philosophia prima sive Ontologia*. Frankfurt and Leipzig, 1730.

WOLTER, Allan B. *The Transcendentals and Their Function in the Metaphysics of Duns Scotus*. New York: St. Bonaventure, 1946.